YOU
ARE
YOUR
Father's
Daughter

Other books by Dr. Earl R. Henslin:

Secrets of Your Family Tree (co-author)

Forgiven and Free: Learn How Bible Heroes
with Feet of Clay Are Models for Your Recovery

Man to Man: Helping Fathers Relate to Sons
and Sons Relate to Fathers

YOU ARE YOUR

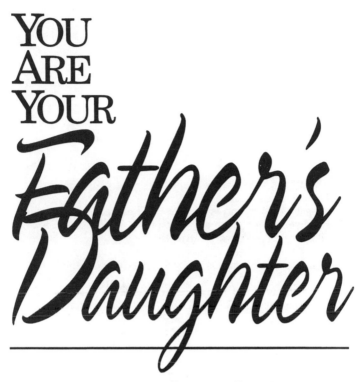

Father's Daughter

DR. EARL R. HENSLIN

THOMAS NELSON PUBLISHERS
Nashville Atlanta London Vancouver

Published in Nashville, Tennessee, by Thomas Nelson, Inc.

Library of Congress Cataloging-in-Publication Data

Henslin, Earl R.
    You are your father's daughter / Earl R. Henslin.
        p.   cm.
    ISBN 0-8407-7722-1
    1. Fathers and daughters—United States.   2. Fatherhood—
Religious aspects—Christianity.   I. Title.
HQ755.85.H458   1994
306.874'2—dc20   94-20711
                                                            CIP

Dedication

To Rachel, Amy, and Jill

Rachel, I respect and admire the young woman you are becoming. Your sensitivity and creativity is far beyond what mine was at your age.

Amy, you are a delightful little girl. You are so excited about everything you are learning in your first years in school.

Jill, you are playful, spunky, so very much alive. May you always feel safe with that precious part of you and never lose it.

To each of you, I am sorry for the times I have failed you, for the times when I have not been there for you. May our heavenly Father guard, keep, and bless you. He has given each of you many gifts and abilities. May He provide you with a strong community of women with whom you can grow and flourish.

I love you,
Dad

ACKNOWLEDGMENTS

I would like to thank Karen for loving me, encouraging me, and supporting me through this project. I am also grateful to my good friend, Will Hawkins, M.D., for his support through daily prayer and encouragement. I thank Bob and Pauline Bartosch for their support and their living example of how two parents in recovery can impact generations. I also appreciate my friends Vance and Bethyl Shepperson, Sam and Judy Doolittle, Royce and Joanie Huitain, Tom and Marcy Dunn, Fred and Joan Mickelson, and Keith and Andrea Miller who offered support and encouragement for this project.

I thank my pastor, Chuck Swindoll, for God has used him to show me how to look deeply into the Scriptures for the road to healing. I also thank pastors Dave Carder, John Columbe, Gary Richmond, and Buck Buchanan who have offered their support and encouragement as friends.

I owe a deep thanks to those who have helped make this book possible. My editor at Nelson, thank you for shepherding it through development. Stephen and Amanda Sorenson, I thank you for your guidance in writing and editing this book. Terri Lopez, I thank you for the miracle of keeping my life organized so that this project could be completed.

Finally, I thank the many women who have survived deep woundedness and allowed me to participate in their healing journey. I honor and respect you. Through your hurt, God has taught me much about His faithfulness, love, grace, and miracle of healing.

CONTENTS

1 The Gift of a Father *1*
Every daughter has a deep, God-given need to be nurtured by a father.

2 Wounded by the Father *17*
No earthly father is perfect, and every daughter suffers pain as a result of that imperfect relationship.

3 Wounded by Life *35*
Many aspects of life are wounding, but a father can do much to help his daughter bear those wounds.

4 Building Healthy Boundaries *55*
A father plays a crucial role in nurturing the development of his daughter's boundaries.

5 Living in the Real World *79*
A father plays a crucial role in enabling his daughter to face the difficult realities of life.

6 Developing Feminine Strength *102*
A father plays a crucial role in nurturing his daughter's feminine strength.

7 The Nurturing Father *120*
Mordecai provides an inspiring example of how a father nurtures his daughter to maturity.

8 **Facing the Loss, Healing the Wounds** *132*
Wounded daughters can find healing and fulfill their God-given potential.

9 **Forgiving Dad** *155*
How a daughter walks through the process of restoring an emotional and spiritual connection with her father.

10 **When Dad Wants to Connect** *178*
How a father can rebuild the emotional and spiritual bridge to his daughter.

11 **Hope for a Healing Community** *194*
How the community of Christian women can promote healing and nurture the development of biblical womanhood.

Notes *207*

CHAPTER 1

The Gift of a Father

Every daughter has a deep, God-given need to be nurtured by a father.

Long ago, a mighty empire stretched from the banks of Pakistan's Indus River westward to the seacoast nations of the Mediterranean. It dominated all of eastern Mediterranean civilization from the eastern-most fringe of Greece south and west into present-day Libya. It stretched from the Aral and Caspian seas in the North southward to the upper reaches of the Nile in present-day Egypt and Sudan. Unsurpassed in greatness and wealth, this massive empire was known as the Persian Empire, and Xerxes was its king.

To celebrate his reign, King Xerxes gave a tremendous party for every nobleman, prince, military leader, and official in the empire. For a full six months he showed off the wealth and greatness of his kingdom. To culminate the festivities, he gave an elaborate banquet that lasted for seven days. Every man was given as much wine as he wanted to drink—the bar was open from morning until night.

Even this was not enough. On the seventh day, when the king was in high spirits from the wine, he wanted something more. He wanted his queen, Vashti, to make an appearance. Vashti was a truly beautiful woman, and the king wanted to show off her beauty to his friends and noblemen. She was one more prize to display for his admirers.

Queen Vashti, however, would have nothing to do with this proposal. More than likely she had been around her drunken husband and his princes before. No self-respecting woman would subject herself to the humiliation of parading before an assembly of drunken men. Drunken men do not say affirming or encouraging things to beautiful women; they usually act out their lust. So, fearful of her own dignity, she refused to come.

What a furor her refusal raised! The king became enraged. He brought together the seven wisest and highest-ranking noblemen in the entire empire and asked them what to do. These men did not like the fact that Queen Vashti had expressed her feelings. They feared that women throughout the empire would soon follow her example. "This very day the Persian and Median women of the nobility who have heard about the queen's conduct will respond to all the king's nobles in the same way," they cautioned. "There will be no end of disrespect and discord."

So the king and his advisors determined that he should publicly divorce Queen Vashti, thereby making her an example to all the women of the empire. "Let the king give her royal position to someone else who is better than she," they advised. "Then when the king's edict is proclaimed throughout all his vast realm, all the women will respect their husbands, from the least to the greatest." The king *followed through with the plan, and he and his nobles were very pleased with their solution. Soon the message went out throughout the land that women needed to listen to their husbands—or else!*[1]

It is easy to see that the Persian Empire was not an easy or safe place for women to live. A woman's outward beauty was viewed as a source of pleasure for men, while her inner person was regarded as insignificant. Yet this is the world into which Esther was born.

Early in her life, both of Esther's parents died, which put her in a perilous position. Women at that time had few opportunities to survive on their own. Esther most likely was left unprotected without land or money—much like Ruth and Naomi, who survived because Ruth gleaned the fields daily, picking up whatever bits of grain the harvesters left behind. Perhaps even more threatening was the fact that even when she was quite young, Esther was recognized as being exceptionally beautiful. In a culture in which harems abounded, physical beauty placed a woman at great risk. Furthermore, Esther was a Jew, a member of a despised race that was viewed as undeserving of respect. Under these conditions, her chance for survival was slim at best.

Then Esther was given a great gift that made all the difference in her life. She was blessed by the gift of Mordecai, a cousin who took her into his family and became her father. The Bible says, "Mordecai had taken her as his own daughter when her father and mother died."[2]

Can you feel the impact of this statement? Try to imagine what it meant for Esther—who had no protection, no future, no hope—when Mordecai took her into his family *as his own daughter.* Mordecai reached out to Esther and took her under his care, guidance, and protection. In so

---

doing, he saved her from a life of certain destitution or the fate of a prostitute or slave.

Esther desperately needed a father. She lived in a dangerous culture. She clearly was at great risk. She needed an older man to step into her life and protect, nurture, and guide her.

Although some external circumstances have changed, women today are also at risk. It is true that women today have achieved a degree of self-sufficiency and have acquired legal protection that was not available to Esther, but, underneath the surface, today's culture is just as dangerous for women as Esther's culture was. One out of four women alive today will experience sexual assault in her lifetime. Despite the sexual revolution, women are objectified today more than ever. This is evident in advertising, television programming, contemporary art and literature, as well as in many male/female relationships. More and more women, in an effort to demand dignified and respectful treatment, are filing sexual harassment suits. Clearly, women today have just as great a need for a loving father as Esther had.

The Need for a Father

It is normal for every person, male or female, to need a father. I believe that's the way God wired us. It's natural for every human being to want to feel the presence of a loving father, to want to be close to a father. It is our human condition to hunger for a father's support, understanding, and comfort. That hunger for a father is an important part of who we are. We see evidence of this hunger all the way back in Old Testament times.

Consider the story of Jacob and Esau.[3] His father's blessing was so important to Jacob that he went to extreme lengths to ensure that he would receive it. His brother Esau was a broken man when he realized that his father's blessing had been taken away from him.

Consider also the story of Joseph.[4] Why did Joseph, who had all the power and wealth any person could want, want so much to know that his father was well and to see his face again? He went to great lengths to break through the denial in his family, to ensure that it was safe enough to reveal who he was, and to ask that his father be brought to him. When his oldest brother, Judah, spoke of their father's love for his sons, Joseph wept so loudly that his sobs could be heard by everyone in his household and in Pharaoh's household as well!

Consider, too, the story of Cain and Abel.[5] Abel's offering of fatty meat from the firstborn of his flock was favorably accepted by his heavenly Father. Cain's offering of the fruit of the land was not. Cain was angry and depressed because his offering to his heavenly Father was rejected. Although God told Cain exactly how to give an acceptable offering, Cain never recovered from his anger. He eventually killed Abel, whose offering God had accepted.

The need we have to feel the presence and love of a father is powerful. During the past few years we have begun to recognize the need for a son to be touched by the emotional and spiritual life of his father. Primarily through the men's movement, we have become aware of the need for a father to build an emotional bridge to his son. Sadly, when this bridge does not exist, a man is deeply wounded. He has a great emptiness in his soul that longs to be filled. That emptiness impacts every area of his life. Although far less attention has been given to it, women carry a similar wound.

The truth is, there is a slot inside every human soul, female as well as male, that needs to be filled through a deep relationship with a father. (There is also a slot that needs to be filled through a deep relationship with a mother, but here we will focus on the need for a father.) There is no denying the need for a father. The need for mother and father relationships has been documented even in infancy. Babies know the difference between their fathers and mothers by the time they are two or three months old. This is especially true of girls, who become attached to their fathers earlier than boys. Although both boys and girls attach to their mothers before they attach to their fathers, all babies need their fathers just as much as their mothers by the time they are eight months old.[6]

In the depths of her soul, a daughter truly needs her father. She needs him from infancy through adulthood. No matter what her age, she needs to feel that she is precious to him. She needs to feel that he loves her, that he will protect her, encourage her, and sacrifice for her. She longs for her father's approval and affirmation of her whole person—her abilities, interests, accomplishments, and inner feelings. I haven't yet met a woman of any age who doesn't want to hear the words, "I'm proud of you," from her father's lips or to have her father put his arm around her when she is hurting.

Tragically, most fathers don't feel their own deep emotional and spiritual needs, so they are unable to recognize and meet these needs in their daughters. In addition, many men have never learned to express their feelings straightforwardly and have difficulty demonstrating their love physically. As a result, their daughters are wounded and carry that woundedness through all of life.

The hunger for healing of that deep wound is so strong that it often dictates the course of a daughter's life. It dictates how she views herself professionally and how she functions with men in the workplace. It dictates her intimate relationships with men—whether or not she will marry, the kind of man she will marry, and the course of her marriage. It dictates how she handles the difficult realities of life such as how she responds to failure, how well she pursues opportunity, how she faces her fears and worries, and how strong she will be when confronted by the physical and emotional threats of living in a dangerous culture.

When healing for that wound does not occur, a woman will try to ease her pain in a number of ways. Overachievement, underachievement, eating disorders, drug and alcohol abuse, sexual and food addictions, and codependency are all common issues that can grow out of a deep woundedness in a woman's relationship with her father. She may also develop unrealistic expectations for the men to whom she relates. She may fantasize about a great white knight in a red Mercedes who is all-loving, all-caring, and will rescue her from her problems. She may have such a deep longing to be touched or held by a man that she seeks physical closeness with male authority figures. All of these responses, and more, come out of the heart of the wounded little girl within the woman who desperately seeks the love, affirmation, and approval that she never received from her father.

The Gift of the Father

As we've seen, Esther was very fortunate that Mordecai took her in and raised her as his daughter, as a member of his family. Mordecai was a wise man. A Jew living in captivity, he was well aware of the ways of the world and possessed a wisdom that most likely was born out of personal pain and difficulty. As Esther's father, he was in no way naive about his family's and daughter's situation. He not only gave Esther physical protection and care but played a very special role in her life, a role that every father can and needs to play. Let's see how the story of Mordecai, King Xerxes, and Esther progresses:

> After a while, King Xerxes missed Queen Vashti. His servants and close officials were concerned. The last thing they wanted was for the king to remember who had suggested that he send Vashti away! So they proposed a search for a suitable replacement.
>
> "Let a search be made for beautiful young virgins for the king," they suggested. "Let the king appoint commissioners in every province of his realm to bring all these beautiful girls into the harem at the citadel of Susa. . . . Then let the girl who pleases the king be queen instead of Vashti."
>
> The king liked this idea, and soon the proclamation went out through the whole empire. This was serious business! No one dared to stand in the way of King Xerxes. If he wanted a new queen, he was going to get one. Notice what happens next.
>
> "When the king's order and edict had been proclaimed, many girls were brought to the citadel of Susa . . . Esther also was taken to the king's palace and entrusted to Hegai, who had charge of the harem."
>
> Esther was taken out of Mordecai's household, but she was not beyond his influence. "Esther had not revealed her nationality and family background, because Mordecai had forbidden her to do so. Every day he walked back and forth near the courtyard of the harem to find out how Esther was and what was happening to her."[7]

My heart wants to burst with the significance of how Mordecai related to Esther when she was taken into King Xerxes' harem. Mordecai loved Esther deeply enough that he taught her how to survive in a dangerous culture. He had enough of an emotional bridge to her that when he told her not to tell anyone who she really was, she could trust the wisdom of his words and walk in the security of his teaching.

Even when Esther was out of Mordecai's sight and protection, she was never out of his mind. Day after day, he walked back and forth, watching and waiting for news of her. He took steps toward his daughter to see how she was faring. Instead of waiting until she desperately needed his help, he stepped toward her. He remained as available to her as he could be, ready to offer her whatever he had to give.

Through this story, which we will study in greater depth, Mordecai gives us a beautiful picture of what it means to be a father to a daughter. It is a great tragedy that more women today do not have fathers who relate to them in the way Mordecai related to Esther. So many women have been terribly wounded by their fathers; they do not have fathers who are safe to be with, much less fathers who can and will lovingly instruct them in how to survive and thrive in a dangerous world.

It is no secret that a loving, feeling father who has an emotional and spiritual connection to his daughter is a lifelong gift to her. If a daughter has the support and affirmation of her father, she will have a much easier time developing her full potential in all areas of life. Psychologist Charles Scull describes in today's terms what the gift of the father means to a daughter:

> A father is the first and often the longest connection a daughter will have with a man. The father-daughter bond (or lack of bond) shapes her future relationships . . . and influences how she moves out in the world.
>
> If he encourages her efforts to achieve, inspires her budding self-confidence, and teaches her competency skills, she will more easily develop an authentic self-esteem. If he discourages her efforts, undermines her self-confidence, shames her body, or discounts her personal opinions, her self-esteem will be marred, and it may take many years for her to learn to believe in herself.[8]

A father builds an emotional bridge to his daughter by learning how to be sensitive to his daughter's heart and being interested in what is important to her. Unfortunately, many fathers don't realize that it is important to pay attention to their daughters' interests. They may not know anything about their daughters' interests, much less take the effort to learn about them, encourage them, or participate in them. Or, some well-meaning fathers try to correct or improve their daughters' efforts to such an extent that they become critical rather than supportive of their daughters' accomplishments. If a father doesn't understand that his daughter's interests come from deep within her heart, he may ignore a vital part of who she is. All of these approaches wound a daughter.

Whether they intend to or not, fathers also define masculinity for their daughters. By the way they relate to their daughters, fathers communicate something about the way all men are. If a father is abusive, manipulative, or controlling, a little girl may grow up feeling that all men are supposed to be that way. If he treats her like a princess, catering to her every whim, she may expect to be pampered by all men. If he expects her to take care of him, she may believe that her role in life is to take care of men. In any of these cases, the daughter may grow up with unrealistic expectations of men and/or a distorted view of her place in the world of men. These misconceptions leave her ill-equipped to survive and prosper.

The view of masculinity that a woman learns from her father also influences how she views God. It is the parent's job to connect with a daughter so that she can grow into the woman God would have her become. Thus the way in which a father relates to his daughter plays a formative role in her spiritual life. In many ways, an earthly father mirrors the attributes of God the Father through his relationship with his daughter. Whether or not he is aware of it, an earthly father gives his daughter her first taste of the heavenly Father.

When a father does not build much of an emotional bridge to his daughter, she may find it difficult to trust what he tries to teach her about life and about God. His words may not feel genuine to her because of the wound in their relationship. If a daughter's heart is not safe in the hands of her earthly father, she may find it difficult to open her heart to her heavenly Father. It is not easy for a daughter to trust that her heavenly Father is safe if her earthly father is not.

Yet when the emotional and spiritual bond between a father and his daughter is strong, the father's presence can provide a much-needed sense of security. An emotionally connected relationship with her earthly father is a constant reminder to a daughter that God the heavenly Father is never very far away. So the emotionally connected father provides an unfailing "God on earth" type of assurance that is present during the best of times and the worst of times. That security of the earthly father's presence and the heavenly Father's presence can be a powerful springboard from which a daughter can step out into new territory and take risks. In this way, a father is truly a great gift.

Being a Father Isn't Easy

It is easy to see that the gift God intended fathers to be in their daughters' lives is an awesome role. It is a role that most men are unprepared to fill. Most men today grew up believing that the primary job description of a father was to provide for his family. A good father worked long hours to meet his family's material needs. He went to the kids' games or performances when he could, tried not to be too physical in his discipline, and made sure the kids went to church. If he accomplished that much, he was considered to be a good father.

Today life is different. The meaning of fatherhood has broadened. We are beginning to realize that the scope of a father's job description is far greater than we assumed it was. Fathers are expected to meet not only financial needs, but emotional and spiritual needs as well. Fathers are confronted by an array of relational expectations that often seem foreign to them. Fathers are expected to be "emotionally connected" to their wives and children. They are expected to "recover" from their own "dysfunctional" family backgrounds. They are expected to deal with their own "woundedness," "codependency," and "addictions." And they are expected to do this with the "support" of other men. (This is all in addition to working out at least an hour a day, participating in Bible studies, having a powerful prayer life, and reading and memorizing God's Word!)

The "old" job description for a father was certainly much easier than the new one. Men can only hope to fulfill their new job description through the empowerment of the Holy Spirit and the support of other men in recovery. Although it is not easy, the father's job description must change so that today's sons and daughters will be equipped with the spiritual and emotional tools they need to survive and thrive in an increasingly dangerous world.

The greatest difficulty to overcome is the fact that a father cannot build emotional and spiritual connections to his children unless he is connected to his own emotional and spiritual life. A father cannot make that connection unless his father has made such a connection—built an emotional and spiritual bridge—to him. Masculine emotion is learned primarily through relationship with the father. Therefore, a father needs to face his own pain and grief for what he missed out on in his relationship with his father so that he can learn how to respond to his children on an emotional and spiritual level. That is why I am such a strong advocate of recovery and healing of the father wound for men. When men are able to face their own grief and loss, they become able to respond to their children, their daughters, on an entirely different emotional and spiritual level.

I have seen this clearly in my own life. I have two older children and two younger children. Although I dearly love each of my children, I have a deeper and more intimate connection with the two younger ones than I was able to have with my two older children when they were young. I have experienced my own recovery for a longer period of time now, which enables me to be more emotionally responsive to my children today than I was years ago. Now, when I come home from work, my three-year-old daughter runs toward the door as soon as she hears my keys jingle in the lock. With a smile on her face and hair flying, she runs down the hall at full speed, yelling, "Daddy, Daddy, Daddy!" When I sweep her into my arms, she buries her head deeply into my chest and says, "Daddy! My Daddy!" Then she holds on real tight. I experience and respond to that connection between us more now than ever before. I am better able today to build an emotional bridge to my children than I was five or ten years ago.

If daughters are to be nurtured by fathers who are fully involved emotionally and spiritually, it is vitally important for fathers to deal with their own grief and to grow through their own recovery. Even so, it is no easy thing to father a daughter. The world of the daughter is different from the world of boys. Fathers know boys. With boys, fathers are in familiar territory, but girls are a puzzle. Fathers prefer boys to girls by a four to one margin, and some men actually grieve that they have a daughter rather than a son.[9] Other men feel confusion when they learn they have become the father of a daughter. Many men just don't know what to do with girls, particularly when their daughters begin to move into adolescence.

Sadly, this confusion and lack of knowledge is very

wounding to daughters. It is no secret that families with sons are less likely to divorce than families with daughters.[10] Even when the family remains intact, a daughter may sense that her father is uncomfortable with her or distances himself from her. The daughter then assumes that she is in some way defective and unworthy of her father's attention and heart. Yet a daughter's need for an emotional and spiritual connection with her father is just as great as the son's need for a similar connection.

To make matters even more difficult, men have few models of how a father can build an emotional bond with his daughter. Fathering a daughter on this level is new. Just this past summer my father, who is in his sixties and is now discovering the importance of being emotionally connected, admitted to my sister, "When you were growing up, I did not know how to relate to women." This is true of many men in my father's generation. It is a new thing for younger men as well. I recently explained to my oldest daughter that this father/daughter stuff is new to me. "Well, Dad," she said, "you do a pretty good job. You have your days, but you do a good job." That's the best a father can do —take one step at a time, one day at a time, and discover his own feeling life so that he can open his heart to his daughter's need for him.

When a father begins to recognize and feel his own emotional life, he becomes more comfortable with his daughter. He can realize that she needs him just as much as a son does. He is better able to realize that a daughter is a person who has needs and feelings just like a son does. After all, when you think about it, there are more similarities than differences in fathering daughters and sons. Both a daughter and a son need time with the father. They both need the father's protection. They both need to experience the playful, fun side of their father. They both need an emotional bridge to their father's heart.

No Father Can Be Everything

When a father realizes the role God has ordained for him to play in his daughter's life, he can easily feel overwhelmed. But God does not intend a father to be anything more than a father. A father can only fill the hole in a daughter's heart that a father can fill. He can't do what the mother needs to do. He can't do what grandparents need to do. He can't do what aunts and uncles need to do. He can't do what the spiritual and professional mentors in his daughter's life need to do. He simply can't do everything. No individual man (or woman) can possibly meet every need a daughter has as she grows from infancy through adulthood.

For example, a daughter learns from her father something of what it means to be feminine, but she doesn't learn everything from him. Her mother also plays a vital role in the development of her feminine identity. A daughter needs female as well as male mentors as she progresses through adult life. These mentoring relationships can be very valuable and offer the daughter a strength and perspective that she could not gain from her father or her mother. A daughter also needs to develop strong, supportive relationships with other women who provide her primary support for whatever load she carries through life.

In the midst of all these relationships, the father has a unique role. He can't be everything, but he can be a constant. He can be there no matter what turns his daughter's life takes. He can be available to listen to her heart and take an interest in her world. He can be alongside her as she discovers how to function in the world with her unique blend of needs, interests, and abilities. He can keep his eyes open and prepare her to face potential pitfalls in her life and relationships. And he can be there to offer support and assurance when his daughter reaches out to him.

In describing the father's role, please understand that I am in no way minimizing the role of the mother. A daughter needs a mother who is spiritually strong, connected to her feelings, and able to respond to the needs of her daughter's heart. A daughter is most blessed if she has a mother *and* a father who love the Lord, love each other, and are committed to a spiritual journey of healing here on earth. Both mother and father have a vital contribution to make to a daughter's life. However, I especially want fathers to realize that just as Mordecai was a gift to Esther, they can be a gift to their daughters.

Questions

1. In what ways are you and your father similar to Esther and Mordecai?

2. In what ways would you desire you and your father to be like Esther and Mordecai?

3. Through your life, when or where have you felt the deepest need for a father?

4. How have you sought to meet the needs that have not been met through your relationship with your father?

5. Take a few moments to honestly evaluate your relationship with your father. Thank God for the times your father has been a gift to you. If you have never known your father, thank God that He is the perfect father.

CHAPTER 2

Wounded by the Father

No earthly father is perfect, and every daughter suffers pain as a result of that imperfect relationship.

I know my father loved me. He worked hard and provided everything for us. I am so thankful for that. Yet he could never say he loved me. He could never just put his arm around me and let me know that I was important to him. He would come home from work anxious and irritable, and I knew that I needed to stay far away from him. When he relaxed after a couple of drinks, things were calmer, but it was often the calm before the storm. I never told my dad a thing about me. He never asked.

☙

My father was a successful, powerful businessman who was respected by everyone at church. My tears, fears, and worries were insignificant to him. And my mom was just overwhelmed by his strength. When I got pregnant at age seventeen, I was nothing but an embarrassment to him. He said I needed to get married and be a mother. He said he would never pay a penny to send me to college. I felt so much pain from the pregnancy that I gave up and married even though I knew it was the wrong thing to do. So I've been a single parent for years, and I don't want anything to do with men. To this day my father will not talk to me. I try real hard, but I will never please him. I can't please God either. Deep inside, I'm afraid that God doesn't really love me.

My father was an alcoholic and molested me when I was six years old. He managed to hide all of his secret sins from his coworkers and from the church. I had sex with the first boy I dated. Even today I cannot say, "NO!" I am married, but I have no boundaries with men. I am sexually addicted and have had one affair after another. How can God love someone like me?

My dad was a pastor. A child in a minister's family quickly learns that there is a different set of rules for the pastor's kids. I was always well behaved, obedient, and nice, but how I hated being an example to others. I could never be real. I couldn't worry. I couldn't be afraid. I couldn't let anybody know how horribly insecure I felt. When a Sunday school teacher touched me where he shouldn't, I felt so bad. I felt like I had failed my father. But he didn't even notice that I wasn't the same person anymore. He had time for others, but he didn't have time for me. Now my relationship with my husband is filled with conflict, and I know why. I expected him to take the place of my father, which is more than any husband can give.[1]

These words from the hearts of wounded daughters provide a glimpse of how important it is for a daughter to have an emotionally connected relationship with her father. It isn't difficult to feel the pain these women carry in their hearts. It isn't difficult to see the depth of a daughter's hunger for a relationship with her father. Sadly, many women have been denied the gift of an emotionally and spiritually connected relationship with their fathers. As a result, they are wounded in ways similar to those described above, and they bear the burden of those wounds for a lifetime. I believe it is time to recognize the impact of the father-daughter relationship and to take steps toward healing the wounds that result from that imperfect relationship.

The women I have had the privilege to work with in psychotherapy have taught me much about how a woman's relationship with her father impacts her personal development and every aspect of her life. Much of psychology has focused on the mother's role in her daughter's psychological and spiritual development, almost to the point of viewing the father as a peripheral figure. Through my work, however, I have come to realize that the father also plays a tremendously significant role in his daughter's development. Much of how a woman views herself is dictated by men. Men greatly influence her view of her potential, capabilities, identity, and spirituality, and her father is the most powerful of those influences.

Loss of the Father

The family in which the father is willing and able to seek out the daughter and build an emotional and spiritual bridge to her is a highly functional family. Unfortunately, most families function at a far-less-than-perfect level. Typically, the father hasn't experienced his own emotional life well enough to recognize and respond to his daughter's emotional needs, so he doesn't build an emotional and spiritual bridge to his daughter. As a result, the daughter suffers a great loss deep in her soul. She feels this wound as a profound sense of loss or deep sadness.

The loss of an emotionally connected relationship between father and daughter can occur in a number of ways. Consider the following examples of how this loss occurs:

- Most fathers work outside the home and may only be physically present (and awake) in the home for a few hours a day. Even when the father is physically present, he may not be emotionally present. Yet it is his emotional presence—the emotional and spiritual connection he has with his daughter—that touches the need of her heart.
- If a girl's parents divorce, the father is likely to see his daughter every other weekend at best and may drop out of her life completely. This abandonment wounds the daughter greatly.
- When a father dies while his daughter is still young, a gaping wound is left in her heart. She needs to feel the physical protection and care that can only come from her father. She needs to be nurtured by a parental voice other than that of her mother. She needs to experience masculine as well as feminine strength. Although the mother can help the daughter deal with this loss, there is simply no way she can fill that void in her daughter's heart.
- A daughter may miss out on an emotionally connected relationship with her father because of his addictions. No matter what the addiction—food, work, sex, drugs, alcohol—it is the addiction, not the daughter, that commands the attention of the father's heart. So the daughter of an addicted man is emotionally and spiritually abandoned, even though her father may be physically present.
- A father may also feel such intense pain from his own unresolved issues that he comes across as cold, defen-

sive, or brusque and is unable to recognize his daughter's pain because he must work so diligently to avoid feeling his own pain.

- A controlling father may shatter the bridge to his daughter's heart in a wide variety of ways. His need to control who she is, what she thinks, or how she behaves attacks her personal identity. By his control, he may violate or deny her intellect, spirituality, integrity, physical ability, or sexuality, as well as her emotions.
- Obviously, a daughter who is physically, emotionally, or sexually violated by her father suffers an incalculable loss. An abusive father has not only failed to build a bridge to his daughter's heart, he has destroyed the very foundation of the bridge. He has created an emptiness that feels as if it can never be filled and an inner terror that nothing can comfort for very long.

The tragedy is, the daughter usually can't identify the nature or source of her loss; she may feel only a vague sense that something is wrong with her. So she may try to be pretty enough, athletic enough, thin enough, smart enough, sexy enough, successful enough, or even try to be the opposite of these characteristics in order to gain her father's attention. She strives for his attention in the hope of gaining his acceptance, approval, and—ultimately—his emotional involvement. There is a catch, however. A daughter is powerless to make an emotional connection with her father; he must initiate that connection. The pain of this lack of emotional connection with her father sets the daughter up for a toxic way of living.

When her inborn hunger for a father remains unfilled, a woman often searches for a father in many other places. She may seek to fill that wound through her work, her marriage, her relationships with authority figures, various addictions, or even involvement in church activities. But there is no way she can find another father who can fill the void left by her birth father. All her attempts to do so will only lead to greater pain and increase the impact of toxic behaviors in her life. To better understand this, let us consider how the quality of the emotional and spiritual relationship that exists between a father and daughter impacts every aspect of the daughter's life.

Impact of the Father Wound on a Woman's View of Her Appearance

I am amazed by how early in life a daughter needs to be acknowledged and appreciated by her father. My youngest daughter, before she was even two years old, already needed me to acknowledge her physical appearance. When she was getting dressed or having her hair combed, she would beam when I told her how nice she looked. When she dressed up in her diapers and draped one of her mother's necklaces around her neck, she was absolutely delighted when I noticed and told her she was pretty.

A daughter needs this kind of affirmation from her father. A loving and emotionally involved father does so much to affirm his daughter's personal identity and nurture her self-confidence. He gives her an important sense of pride and confidence in her personal identity that will enable her to stand strong in a world that will threaten her uniqueness. In our society, a daughter needs this kind of involvement from her father just to handle the pressure of Barbie™ dolls. Our culture has an obsession with large bustlines and perfectly-toned, thin bodies. It places no value on the heart and soul of a person; appearance and image are everything. So it takes a very secure young woman to stand up to the image of the ideal woman she observes on television, in the movies, and in the magazines.

Sadly, many fathers fail to realize how much a daughter

needs her father's affirmation of her physical appearance and how closely she observes his attitudes toward women. A little girl learns very early on what kind of woman draws her father's eyes. If the father turns his head to look after attractive women who pass by, his daughter may develop an extreme body obsession. Her view of herself and how she needs to look may become very distorted. She may strive to be thin enough, glamorous enough, or sexy enough —not so much because she wants other men to notice her, but because she wants her father to notice her. If the father is lustful and/or has a sexual addiction so that he visually undresses women when he looks at them or makes sexual comments about them, the daughter notices and takes his comments to heart. She knows all too well that she is growing into a woman and that her father treats women as objects or as something to play with or laugh at. She may then work doubly hard to please men by her appearance or may seek to protect herself from men by being unattractive.

All too many daughters have looked in the garage for a tool or in their father's desk for a pencil and accidentally discovered his stash of pornography. The daughter looks at the photographs and naturally concludes that this is the kind of woman her father really desires, the kind of woman men want her to be. This wound in the daughter's soul may never be acknowledged, but it will impact her life on a daily basis. Her feelings of inadequacy in trying to live up to the image she sees may lead to a lifetime of struggle with her appearance and weight. This will not only impact her relationships with men, including the man she may marry, but will also affect her ability to instill a sense of personal value and a healthy body image to her own daughter. No woman can communicate a healthy body image to her daughter if she has not learned to accept her own body as it is.

The Impact of the Father Wound on a Woman's Perception of Her Physical Strength

The father plays an important role in affirming not only his daughter's appearance but her strength as well. Daughters hunger for an affirmation of their physical strength. They like to wrestle on the floor with their fathers, just as sons do. They like to hike, swim, climb trees, and ride bikes, and they delight in doing these activities with their fathers.

The wise father will affirm and encourage his daughter's physical strength and ability as she grows up. He has many opportunities to do so: when his daughter takes her first steps, when she tries to climb a tree, when she learns how to ride a bike, when she practices throwing a ball. At these times he can praise her strength and physical ability. As she grows older, father and daughter may participate in even more physical activities. Perhaps they sail or canoe together. Perhaps they swim laps together at a local pool. Perhaps they take a backpacking trip. Perhaps they play tennis. These are just a few of the many physical activities that fathers and daughters can share.

My daughter Rachel and I have enjoyed bike riding together. When she was nine years old, we completed a twenty-five-mile ride on a tandem. When we finished the ride, she stood next to me with her arm around me and said, "We really did that, Daddy!"

"Yes, Rachel," I answered. "We did it all the way. All twenty-five miles!"

Rachel received a T-shirt for completing the ride, and she wore it proudly. She told her friends and neighbors (adults, too) that she had completed a twenty-five-mile ride. People couldn't believe that a nine-year-old girl had ridden that far. It is important that a daughter receive the message that she is physically capable and strong. Her father plays a vital role in communicating that message, which is as important to her well-being as his affirmation of her appearance.

Impact of the Father Wound on a Woman's Need for Physical Affection

In addition to receiving affirmation of her physical strength and capability, a daughter needs to experience appropriate physical closeness with her father. When a father playfully tousles his young daughter's hair, she feels special to him. When he holds and comforts her when she scrapes her knee, she feels safe and loved. When he gives his teenage daughter a congratulatory pat on the shoulder, she feels confident and encouraged. These expressions of physical closeness do much to strengthen a daughter's confidence and self-assured identity.

The father is intended to be the "safe" man from whom a daughter learns about appropriate physical boundaries in her relationships with men. But many fathers find it difficult to navigate this area successfully. A father, for example, may in fact violate his daughter's physical and sexual boundaries. This sends a very confusing message to the daughter, leaving her with feelings of shame that devastate her self-confidence. On the other extreme, a father may so fear violating his daughter's boundaries that he will physically withdraw from her, refusing to touch or hug her even when it is appropriate. This, too, is wounding to the daughter.

Either extreme, the violation of abuse or the withdrawal of all physical touch, leaves the daughter with no experience of physical closeness with men and no standard by which to discern appropriate physical touch. This wound in the relationship with the father clearly impacts the daughter's sexuality. It leaves her confused and creates a tendency for her to move toward an oversexualized or under-sexualized extreme.

Some women who have not received appropriate physical affection and comfort from their fathers have a deep *skin hunger*, an aching desire to be held or comforted by a man. This skin hunger is powerful and very confusing. It often plays a role in sex-love addiction as well as in sexual dysfunction. Women who have a skin hunger crave the physical comfort of being close to another warm body. The need to be held feels essential to their survival. Their desire for physical comfort is so strong that these women become involved in relationships with men primarily so they will be held. Then they are genuinely surprised when the relationship becomes sexual. When a man moves from physical closeness toward sexual involvement, these women are powerless to stop the progression. Or, they may feel detached and uninvolved, as if they have no choice about what is happening to them sexually.

Impact of the Father Wound on How a Woman Views Her Role in Life

The way in which a father relates to his daughter not only affects his daughter's personal identity and view of herself, but affects how she views her role in life and how she fits into the world around her. The dynamics of the father-daughter relationship serve as a model and testing ground by which the daughter learns how to relate to men. So the father-daughter relationship has a long-term impact on every aspect of the daughter's life. In some cases the dynamics of their relationship serve the daughter well. In other cases the dynamics yield devastating results.

Psychologists have identified seven distinct types of father-daughter relationships. It is interesting to note that the way in which a father relates to his daughter often results from his own woundedness and pain. Let's consider some of the more common ways father-daughter dynamics play a significant role in the daughter's life.[1]

Princess Daughter Some fathers pamper their daughters, providing every material desire their daughters have. This approach may grow out of the father's own insecurity and fear that he is not lovable, which compels him to try to buy his daughter's love. Or, the father may be cut off emotionally and spiritually and may find it difficult to play with or be emotionally expressive with his daughter. He then gives to her materially because it's the only way he knows how to give. In other cases, the father's addictions—whether they be work, substance abuse, or something else—allow little time for him to be involved with his daughter, so he gives materially as a way of "making up" for what he doesn't give personally.

A daughter who has this kind of father grows up with a "princess" mentality and goes through life expecting all men to pamper her. In personal relationships, she measures her importance according to the gifts she is given: the more expensive the gift, the more loved she feels. In the workplace, she often considers herself to be better than others and expects special treatment and privileges beyond those that are given to her coworkers. Spiritually, she may be inclined to believe that God loves her when all is going well but to doubt His love for her during difficult times. If she marries, her view has a tremendous impact on her marriage.

Many fathers actually feel relieved when a princess daughter marries and moves out of the home. Unfortunately, the man who marries a princess runs head-on into incredible expectations and usually doesn't have a clue about what's in store for him. All he sees is a good-looking woman who dresses beautifully all the time and drives a fancy car, but he has no idea what will be required of him to support that lifestyle. More important, he doesn't realize that his wife will feel betrayed and unloved if he doesn't provide the gifts and material expressions of caring that she is used to receiving.

Angry Daughter A father who feels that he has been wounded by women in the past will reflect that hurt in his relationship with his daughter. He may demand affection and care from her in a way that violates her role as his daughter. This is a type of emotional incest. Or, the father may try to cover up his pain by controlling and exerting power over his daughter.

A daughter who feels frustrated or violated by her father's attempts to mask his pain at her expense will become an angry woman. Anger is her defense. It is the wall she keeps between herself and others whenever she feels threatened or unsafe. Often frightened by closeness or vulnerability, she may have a difficult time discerning between friend and foe. For this wounded and damaged woman, anger becomes a motivating force. It is the means by which she proves her competence and worth.

The angry woman's wound in her relationship with her earthly father is usually evident in her strong rejection of God the Father. She has great difficulty picturing God the Father as loving and compassionate. To her, He is angry and judgmental. In the workplace, her anger is an ever-ready weapon, poised to attack any men who threaten her or get too close. And the man who marries an angry woman literally lives in a mine field. Anywhere he moves may lead to an explosion of her built-up resentment and rage. When her anger explodes, all the husband can do is duck, unless he is crazy enough to rage back. If that happens, the scene is set for a mutually destructive relationship.

Amazon Daughter A father also produces an angry daughter when he makes promises to her and fails to keep them. The promises the father breaks may be promises to do certain activities, commitments to be present for important events in her life, or promises that are inherent in the father-daughter relationship such as the promise of physical, sexual, and emotional safety. If a father breaks the inherent promises of the father-daughter relationship, particularly if he breaks them through abuse or incest, anger—often to the point of rage—results. In fact, extreme anger or rage at the slightest provocation is one sign of an abusive relationship in the past.

When there is abuse (particularly sexual abuse) in the father-daughter relationship, an angry daughter may go a step further and become what can be called an amazon woman. This woman is angry but also has the skills to act on her anger. She doesn't just get mad; she will destroy you at your own game. This woman knows how to survive. She has turned her rage into skills that enable her to compete. But hers is no ordinary spirit of competition; it is competition to the extreme. It is competition that will win—at any cost.

This woman can be ruthless and calculating, which isn't all bad because, to a certain degree, those skills are at times necessary for survival, but she uses them to a destructive extreme. Although she may be a successful entrepreneur, she doesn't know how to be interdependent. She has steeled herself so that inside she has no need for men. The thought of being dependent on anyone is far too frightening for her to consider. If she is married, she often makes more money than her husband. An intimidating force in the workplace, the amazon daughter meets every conflict with a drawn sword—and she rarely loses. Tragically, this woman who has incredible potential for succeeding against all odds usually faces equally powerful feelings of loneliness and isolation.

When I think of this daughter, I think of Major Hoolihan on the old television serial "MASH." In one episode, she berates another nurse for crying for the wounded who died. Hoolihan has no place for a nurse who cries on the job and wants the offending nurse to be transferred to another unit. The other nurses, however, rally around the nurse who cried and share their mutual feelings of laughter as well as tears. Hoolihan is noticeably excluded from their camaraderie. Then a stray dog Hoolihan has befriended dies, and the strong major can take no more. She cries for the dog and cries for all the wounded who died as she tried to save them. Afterward she goes to the other nurses and apologizes. In tears, they open their arms to her and accept her as a warrior with a compassionate heart.

Victim Daughter Anger and ruthless independence are not the only outcomes of abuse in the father-daughter relationship. Rather than becoming angry, some women internalize the message they received from their fathers that they are insignificant and have no rights—not even rights to their own feelings or bodies. They go through life allowing themselves to be dominated, controlled, and abused. They are powerless to set boundaries to protect themselves from abusive relationships, which sets them up to suffer through repeated relationships with abusive men.

In the workplace, victim daughters may overachieve or underachieve, but their deep feelings of being defective or inadequate remain unchanged by their external behavior. Powerful shame issues are often at work beneath the surface, putting these women at high risk for addiction or codependency. Sadly, these women usually have tentative, performance-oriented relationships with God. They feel they must do just the right things so God will not punish them, but they feel empty and inadequate when it comes to a personal relationship with God.

Mother-Earth Daughter While still a child, this daughter learned to survive by taking care of her father or by taking care of her mother because the father wasn't available for either of them. The father (as well as the mother) may project his own helplessness or neediness on the daughter and expect her to heal his wounds. From an early age, the daughter exists to meet the needs of the parent(s) rather than the parent(s) being there to meet her needs. This is a type of emotional incest. Forced into the role of caring for adults at an early age, this daughter has had no childhood. She internalizes the message that if she has needs, she is bad.

The mother-earth daughter learns to be nice, kind, and to take care of everything. A first-class codependent, she is the glue that holds everything together. Companies and churches love her because she sacrifices her life to do whatever impossible tasks she is given. She earns approval by being there for others who need her, but believes that she herself is unworthy of receiving love or care from others.

Inside, the mother-earth daughter may carry tremendous pain from denying her needs and sacrificing her dreams in order to juggle the needs of others. But no one knows her pain. This woman is so used to denying her needs that she may find it very difficult to identify the needs at the root of her pain. If she were able to identify those needs, her underlying belief that her feelings are unimportant would make it difficult for her to share those needs with another person. So she carries her pain alone.

Yearning Daughter Sometimes a father has a tremendous lack of confidence, especially when it comes to having a warm, close relationship with his daughter. He doesn't know how to play with girls and certainly doesn't know what it means to be affectionate and loving to a daughter. When a father feels insecure in his relationship with his daughter, he often holds her at arm's length. He keeps emotional walls between himself and his daughter so she doesn't get too close to him or his insecurities.

The daughter of a distant father may not be aware of what is happening on a conscious level, but she certainly feels the coldness and distance in the way he relates to her. His implied rejection of her settles deep in her soul. She grows up yearning for the closeness she never had with him. As a result, she generally has poor boundaries with other people, especially with men.

Easily overwhelmed, the yearning daughter has a tendency to function at extremes. She may let others take advantage of her, or she may hold others at a distance where they can't hurt her. She may appear to be self-confident and poised, or insecure and fearful. Her yearning for affection and physical closeness may be so strong that she cannot maintain sexual boundaries, or she may try to protect herself by being sexually detached and cold.

In marriage, she may be like a chameleon. Her husband has a difficult time discovering where she is emotionally. She may indicate that it is safe to approach her, but when her husband moves toward her, she becomes insecure, changes her colors, and slips away. Both husband and wife suffer from the woundedness in the father-daughter relationship that dictates the marriage.

In the workplace, the yearning daughter rides an emotional roller coaster. She may doubt the praise that is given to her, or she may accept it and then feel tremendous rejection at the slightest hint of negative feedback. As in all of her relationships, the yearning daughter longs for a secure relationship with God. The difficulty is, she can't trust

God's stability and faithfulness, so it is difficult for her to trust and reach out to Him. She lives on a roller coaster, propelled to experience great fear or ecstatic thrills over which she has no control.

Companion Daughter Some men assume a Pygmalion-type role in fatherhood. In these cases, the daughter becomes the means by which her father creates the perfect daughter who will prove to the world what a great person he is. He may be loving, caring, and supportive toward his daughter, but his motivation is primarily to make himself look good, not to benefit her. As such, he may be unable to support or affirm his daughter if her pursuits don't make him look good. Furthermore, he may even withdraw his love and support if his daughter embarrasses or displeases him. As you might expect, this father's personal worth and value rises and falls with his daughter's performance.

This type of fathering devastates a daughter's self-esteem. She grows up believing that she herself is nothing, that her worth is dependent upon her father's approval. This viewpoint pushes her toward perfectionism and codependency. If she doesn't do just the right things and act in just the right way, she is nothing.

This not only leaves her with an inability to say "no" to her father's needs, it leaves her unable to grow up. Her father's need for her emotional sustenance keeps her bound to him. Unless the father releases her into adult life, she will remain unable to care for her own needs in life and unable to have an emotionally intimate relationship with her husband. She will remain always available to please others in an effort to please her father.

Not all father-daughter relationships fall into these clear categories. Often aspects of several relationship dynamics are at work. And since relationships are never static, the father-daughter dynamics may change over time, particularly if the father or daughter takes steps toward recovery. In any case, these relationship dynamics give us an idea of the significant impact a father has on his daughter's perception of herself and her place in the world. As a father, I am so thankful that my daughters and I also have a heavenly Father to lean on. His presence in our lives offers great healing for the wounds we suffer in relationship with our imperfect, earthly fathers.

Questions

1. Which wounds in your life today have resulted from your relationship with your father?

2. How can you encourage your father to initiate an emotional connection with you? Describe what that emotional connection would be like.

3. How has your relationship with your father impacted your self-image?

4. What losses in your relationship with your father have been most difficult or painful for you?

5. Which of the types of the seven father-daughter relationships describe(s) you and your father?

CHAPTER 3

Wounded
by Life

Many aspects of life are wounding, but a father can do much to help his daughter bear those wounds.

The following true/false statements help identify some of the prevailing attitudes and shaming messages that continue to wound women throughout life. These messages may be conveyed through a woman's family, her church, the workplace, or our culture in general. Feel free to add your own observations to this list!

T   F   The way a woman dresses determines a man's sexual response toward her.

T   F   Eve is responsible for Adam taking a bite out of the forbidden fruit in the Garden of Eden.

T   F   A man's sexual needs are primary, and a woman's sexual needs are secondary.

T F *Men are always right.*

T F *According to God's Word, women are to be submissive to men in all things. They are not to have any thoughts, feelings, or opinions of their own.*

T F *If a woman wants to get a man's attention, she has to have a perfect body, just the right clothes, and a beautiful face.*

T F *Women do not have business and administrative abilities. That is why they should stay at home— out of church, business, and government.*

T F *The words* feminine *and* strength *do not belong together.*

T F *Men become sex addicts, have affairs, or sexually abuse children because their wives are not sexual enough.*

T F *Women should control family finances only when they are single parents or widows.*

T F *It is never right for a woman to say no to her husband's sexual advances.*

T F *Delilah is responsible for Samson losing his hair, strength, and eyesight.*

T F *If a woman would only meet her husband's needs better, he would not be emotionally, physically, or spiritually abusive.*

T F *Women are not as capable as men when it comes to planning military strategy or fighting in combat.*

T F *Women who are physically strong usually aren't very attractive.*

T F *Men think that women who are physically attractive are more intelligent than those who are unattractive.*

T F   *With all those female hormones at work, you never know what a woman is going to do next, and you can't trust what she says about her feelings.*

A quick look at these statements makes it clear that women have to contend with a significant number of destructive messages about being female. This is just a partial list of wounding messages that greatly distort a woman's view of herself and her value before God. A woman who has a weak or nonexistent emotional bridge to her father is easily devastated by these wounding cultural influences. There is no way she can insulate herself from these messages that deepen the wound she already has in her relationship with her father.

The Impact of Wounds from the Culture

Consider for a moment the messages about feminine that are conveyed through television and the advertising media. Much of the mass marketing in our culture is based on sexual addiction. Sex sells everything from perfume to cars, clothing to coffee, and breakfast cereal to diet soft drinks. Sexually oriented advertising not only sells, it sends two very clear messages to women. The first message is that women are supposed to be sexy. The second message is that a woman's desire and ability to meet extreme standards of sexual flamboyance will determine her success in life. Little girls have to grow up with industrial-strength boundaries to stand up against these messages.

These messages don't end with advertising. Much television programming further deepens the wound in a woman's sexual identity. What was considered R rated programming two decades ago is now regular fare on television. Even little children are exposed to sexual abuse and extramarital affairs in daily television viewing. For six to ten hours a day, the message that it is normal for two people to meet, kiss, and make love goes out to anyone who turns on a television. What an example of boundary failure!

Unfortunately, the Christian culture has inflicted wounds on sexual identity as well. Many Christian women were taught that sexuality is shameful rather than a unique part of who God created them to be. Young women who became pregnant were greatly shamed within the church. Some were sent away in order to avoid embarrassing the family or the church. Others had to confess their shameful sin before the whole congregation. Still others fearfully sought secret abortions in an effort to escape the judgment of others. With this shame-filled background, it isn't uncommon to feel sinful for having any sexual feelings. The tragedy is, these distorted messages often govern a woman's sexual experience within her marriage.

The confusing application of certain Christian doctrines has wounded women in other ways as well. Between Eve's first bite of the forbidden fruit and Bathsheba's submission to David's lust, women have often been made to carry an inordinate responsibility for the sins of the world. The teaching that the wife should submit to her husband at all costs—even if he is abusive—has also inflicted deep wounds on women young and old. If there is no spiritual or emotional connection with a loving, feeling father on earth, these wounds are physically and spiritually destructive.

Women are also wounded by the multiple messages that invalidate and suppress the expression of their feelings. When a young woman reaches adolescence and is attracted to a young man, she can't openly express her interest by asking him out on a date. Instead, she has to play the game of trying to attract his attention and hold his interest so that he will ask her out. This doesn't do much to encourage openness and honesty in her relationships with men.

When women do express strong feelings, they are often mocked or criticized. Women who cry are written off as being too emotional or worse, unstable. Women who express anger are called names that men who express anger are not called. Women are even pressured into allowing others to define their emotional state by having the feelings they experience during their premenstrual time dismissed. Although a woman's feelings may be somewhat magnified during her premenstrual time, it certainly doesn't mean that her feelings are not genuine or legitimate. If her father has not taken her feelings seriously from birth, it is terribly difficult for a woman to own her feelings and stand up to the destructive cultural view.

This is by no means an exhaustive list of the ways our culture deepens and intensifies the woundedness women have suffered in relationship with their fathers. Even in its abbreviated form, this list shows how important it is for a father to build an emotional and spiritual bond with his daughter. When she is strengthened by an unbreakable bond to her father's heart, a woman has the resources to stand against these influences and fulfill her potential. But if she lacks that bond, the wound in her relationship with him continues to deepen. Its impact is felt in every area of her life.

Impact of the Father Wound on a Woman's Marriage

When a daughter doesn't receive what she needs from her father emotionally, she may unknowingly seek to fill that need through her relationships with other men, particularly romantic relationships. Yet such relationships are primed for disaster. When a woman has experienced a deep wound in the relationship with her father, she has incredibly high expectations for the man she marries. And the man falls right into it. He feels needed and important because his wife needs him so much. In all likelihood he, too, is wounded, which magnifies the problem. Notice what happens in many serious male/female relationships:

The wounded daughter begins to date a man, and if the dating relationship progresses, she begins to think that she has found the most wonderful man on earth. The little girl inside her thinks, *Yippee! This guy is going to love me all the time. He's going to care for me all the time. He will always be there for me.* But there are two major problems at work in the relationship. First, the biggest share of what the woman is feeling is what she has been looking for in a father. Second, the man is wounded too. The little boy inside him is thinking, *All right! This woman will love and hold and care for me all the time. She thinks I'm wonderful, that I do great things. She will always affirm and adore me.*

What develops between this man and woman is a toxic state called love and romance. When this state of toxic love is going on there is no such thing as premarital counseling because there is no way to address the real issues in the relationship. The truth is, the couple needs a month in detox so they can withdraw from each other and begin to see each other as they really are. Many divorces would be eliminated if we did premarital counseling this way!

All of this is to say that many marriages are based on a shaky foundation of woundedness. The man and woman each live under the burden of unmet needs, and that burden may be so great that it is nearly impossible to recognize the real individuals underneath. The little girl and the little boy inside each of them hopes they have actually found somebody who can love them as no one ever has before. Then, twenty-four hours, six months, or five years into the marriage, things begin to fall apart.

Due to his wounds, the husband may have been cut off

from his feelings for years. The only emotions he really feels are anger, sex, and rejection. When his wife no longer matches his image of the all-magical woman he expected her to be, he may feel rejected and withdraw from her. Then the woman realizes that her husband isn't the all-loving, wonderful man she thought he was. She becomes angry, depressed, and resentful because he isn't what she expected him to be. Although there may well be problems in the marriage, much of her disillusionment with the marriage (and his as well) relates to the hunger for an emotional and spiritual connection with the father. That connection is something a husband can complement but is incapable of providing. The daughter's need for her father must be worked out through her relationship with her father, not her husband.

Impact of the Father Wound on Marriage

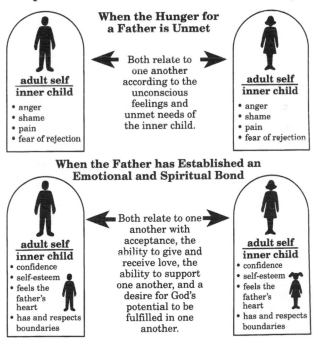

When the Hunger for a Father is Unmet

adult self
inner child

- anger
- shame
- pain
- fear of rejection

Both relate to one another according to the unconscious feelings and unmet needs of the inner child.

adult self
inner child

- anger
- shame
- pain
- fear of rejection

When the Father has Established an Emotional and Spiritual Bond

adult self
inner child

- confidence
- self-esteem
- feels the father's heart
- has and respects boundaries

Both relate to one another with acceptance, the ability to give and receive love, the ability to support one another, and a desire for God's potential to be fulfilled in one another.

adult self
inner child

- confidence
- self-esteem
- feels the father's heart
- has and respects boundaries

Every husband and wife enter into marriage with some emotional needs, some woundedness and hurt. It is part of marriage to meet some of those needs. However, it isn't easy for any one person to meet those needs, and it is even more difficult to find one's way through the deep needs that can and cannot be met through the marriage. A woman who has a solid relationship with her father, however, probably has the best resource available to handle the rigorous ups and downs of marriage and family life.

A woman who has a strong bridge to her father's heart has more to give to her husband. Working through the burdens she and her husband each carry is less of a strain for her because she has the strength of her father's love to support her. This doesn't mean that the father is involved in the marriage in the sense of talking with his daughter about the details of what is happening in the marriage. Rather, his relationship with his daughter and his faithful presence in her life have given her the wisdom, strength, and support that enable her to handle whatever turns her life takes. His daughter does not stand alone; she stands with her father's presence behind her.

The wound in the relationship between father and daughter can impact the daughter's marriage in other ways as well.

When a little girl is wounded by her father, particularly if she has been abused by him, she can't express her anger toward him. (That's like asking for her head to be handed to her.) So the little girl grows up and develops an adult body, but she still carries that anger inside. She marries, and one day an issue arises between her and her husband. Her husband does something—switches his tone of voice, uses a particular phrase, gives her a look, or makes a hand gesture —that is similar to the way her father acted. Boom! The little girl's anger suddenly explodes. She is sure that her husband is the most inconsiderate man in the world. She can't even imagine why she married him. Her only reality is that her husband is the biggest jerk in history. Although her husband may have said or done something insensitive, what is really happening is that he tripped the switch that unleashed the anger she had stored up against her father. So the husband receives all of the anger his wife has ever had toward her father. Obviously this is damaging to the marriage. It isn't possible for this kind of anger and affection to exist at the same time, and it isn't easy for a woman to make a distinction on a feeling level between her husband and her father.

In some cases, a woman who is codependent in her marriage or family relationships may unconsciously be acting out the pain and fear she feels as a result of her relationship with her father. She may become an all-loving, all-caring person who tries to meet the needs of everyone in the family. She may become the self-sufficient woman who does everything on her own without the help of others. She may go to extremes to gain her husband's approval. She may even stay with an abusive husband, always hoping that things will get better—just as she did when she was a little girl. It may take a long time for her to wake up to the fact that the way she handles life isn't normal and that she needs to face the scary emotions she feels inside.

At times the wound in the father-daughter relationship becomes evident through the father and son-in-law relationship rather than through the daughter's behavior. Sometimes the father is so wounded or has such a great need for a son that he essentially abandons his daughter when she marries and brings a new man into the family. The father and his son-in-law may have a great time talking and doing things together. For the most part this is good, but sometimes a father and son-in-law become almost inseparable. If the daughter has not had the benefit of a close relationship with her father, she will be wounded by this. Some women have even expressed fears to me about the future of their marriage because they see their father and husband becoming so close that they feel as if they will lose both of them.

In other situations, a father may be so controlling and involved in his daughter's life that he has a difficult time letting go of his adult daughter and allowing her to develop her marriage relationship. In these cases, the father may be like a shadow, competing against his son-in-law for his daughter's attention. If he feels threatened by his son-in-law's success, he may make it a point to project an image of financial success or give expensive gifts to his daughter. The father may also seek to undermine the marriage relationship by pointing out his son-in-law's faults to his daughter. Although there are times when a father should express to his daughter concern for what is happening in her marriage, he needs to share his concern and leave the decision-making and consequences in his daughter's hands. Adult daughters are responsible to God to make and work through their own choices in life. A father who wants to maintain a relationship with his adult daughter will continue to love her even when he doesn't approve of the choices she makes.

Impact of the Father Wound on Other Relationships

A woman doesn't have to be married in order for the lack of emotional connection with her father to greatly impact her family life. Alicia, for example, is in her thirties but has never married. Both of her parents worked full time, so she literally grew up in day care. Her parents took her out of bed in the morning while she was still in her pajamas and dropped her off at the day care provider's home. The day care provider had so many children to care for that as soon as Alicia was able, she was required to dress herself and prepare her own breakfast cereal. No one was there to help her dress or to sit down and talk with her as she ate breakfast. For as long as she can remember, she took care of herself.

Consequently, Alicia has never had a strong emotional bond with either parent. As an adult, she constantly feels lost and very much alone in everything she does. She is so insecure about where she belongs that she has a hard time staying in a relationship. Now in her second long-term relationship, she cannot bring herself to make a commitment to marry. She's a tough survivor, but that's all she knows how to do. In the absence of a strong emotional connection with her parents, especially with her father, Alicia doesn't know how to go beyond surviving.

Consider, too, what happens in the daughter's heart when her father has an affair. When the daughter finds out that there is another woman in her father's life, she is immediately wounded. It becomes clear to her that the other woman is more important to her father than his wife and his child(ren). When the daughter sees that her dad is alive and happy and wants to spend all of his time with the other woman, she personalizes the situation. The message she receives from her father is this: the other woman is more important to me than you are. This is particularly wounding if the daughter has not personally experienced her father's emotional involvement.

If the affair progresses to the point of divorce and later marriage to the other woman, the daughter suffers an even greater wound. This situation can be particularly devastating if the new wife has children. It is very common for the daughter to see her father become more emotionally involved with his new wife's children than he ever was with her. The daughter may see her father play with his new wife's children with an enthusiasm he never had when he played with her. Even if he is not all that emotionally connected to his new wife's children, his daughter may see him as an all-loving, magical man who cares for his new children, but not for her.

If the daughter of a divorced and remarried father manages to overcome these great obstacles and develop some kind of an involved relationship with him, she then has to deal with her mother. Her mother may be very jealous of her daughter's ongoing relationship with the father and may seek to undermine the father-daughter relationship by criticizing the father or chiding the daughter for wanting to have a relationship with him. This is terribly confusing and wounding to the daughter.

The situation becomes more complex if the daughter's mother remarries. A stepfather can easily become the target of the daughter's unresolved anger and resentment toward her birth father. The stepfather may be a pretty nice guy, but he receives a continual "on again, off again" treatment from the daughter because of the damage done in her relationship with her father.

One man I knew, for example, married a woman with a young daughter. Emotionally and financially, he gave everything he had to his stepdaughter. He was involved with her as she was growing up, put her through college, went shopping with her, and gave her cars, but his involvement has never been appreciated. The daughter is in her late twenties and still lives at home, yet she is angry and resentful of her stepfather. It has finally dawned on him that she has never grown up, does not want to take responsibility for anything, and he has fostered her emotional and financial immaturity.

The reality underlying this scenario is that the mother has never dealt with her father wound, never resolved her feelings concerning the divorce, never addressed her first husband's addiction—and the daughter hasn't addressed these issues either. The result is that the stepfather has allowed himself to pay the price for what did and did not happen in the family (in the relationship with the father), before he entered the picture. It is tragic that the old wounds between father and daughter have played such a significant role in this and many other families.

Impact of the Father Wound in the Workplace

I am amazed by the number of women who have trouble believing in their potential, particularly women who are stuck in low-paying, low-status positions such as office manager or executive secretary yet actually run the companies that employ them. If you take a close look at what many of these women are doing, you realize that although they use the same skills required of the owners and high-level managers, they don't recognize their abilities nor do they receive recognition for them. This is one way in which the father wound affects women in the workplace.

Please don't misunderstand me. I am in no way critical of women in these positions, for there is nothing inherently wrong with these jobs. The issue is not the position, but how a woman views herself in the job she is doing. The unfortunate thing is many women feel inadequate when, in reality, they are highly skilled and extremely capable. As a result, these women lack the confidence necessary to take the risks that will improve their vocational and financial status. They don't believe they could further their education or network to obtain a job that would provide greater recognition and reward for their abilities.

Julia is a good example of this. She grew up in a home where the father ruled with an iron fist accompanied by ample doses of guilt and shame. Her husband was also controlling and abusive—to the point that his addictions eventually bankrupted the family emotionally, spiritually, and financially. Forced to face divorce later in life, Julia needed to find a job. She thought she would look for some kind of routine clerical position, but I encouraged her to seek something more challenging.

"Julia," I said, "you help orchestrate the women's ministry and retreats for a large church. You have raised children, managed a household, and supervised a Sunday school training program. As far as I know, those are the skills needed to manage a small company. Don't limit yourself to a clerical job."

Julia still wasn't sure of her abilities, so she started as a part-time secretary at a college. She continued her recovery program and when a position as coordinator of campus activities became available, she applied for it and was hired. In her new job she scheduled classes, seminars, and other activities for the whole college. Soon the director of a large camp noticed her abilities and offered her a job as activities coordinator for the camp. She now works at the camp and has a house to live in plus a good salary with benefits.

It is sad when a woman has all the brain power, gifts, and abilities she needs but feels inadequate to take the risks that will enable her to live up to her God-given potential. I see a very different picture when a woman has some kind of an emotional connection with her father. Women who have that connection with their fathers have much greater confidence that they can take risks and step into new areas of growth. So the father's encouragement and support of his daughter as she grows up is no small thing.

How does a father nurture this confidence in his daughter? The process starts while his daughter is still a little girl. It starts when he helps her learn new things. It happens when he praises her accomplishments. It builds when he lets her know that he is confident of her abilities. It deepens as he encourages her to pursue new areas of interest.

This is a role the father plays throughout his daughter's

life. It does not end when she leaves home. It is important that a father remain active enough in his adult daughter's life to continue to encourage her, while at the same time respecting her enough to avoid becoming overinvolved in her life. It is helpful for him to know what his daughter does and how she views her work. Then, when she dreams about a future goal, he can provide some perspective on what the fulfillment of those dreams might require of her and what the benefits might be. His confident support can encourage her to take the chances to do what she really wants to do.

On the other hand, an abusive father will greatly magnify a woman's lack of confidence. This lack of confidence may or may not be obvious. Some women believe they are inadequate and seem to live their lives proving that. Other women have a deep sense of inadequacy that compels them to overachieve. Women in this latter group are driven to perform far beyond what is expected. They are usually successful in meeting their goals but rarely experience pleasure or satisfaction in their accomplishments. Their achievement is born more out of a fear of failure than out of a desire to succeed. Those fears can be powerful, even to the point of propelling her into addictive work patterns. No amount of work or financial security will fill the emptiness her father has left in her heart.

When a woman lacks the assurance of her father's love and confidence in her, she is set up to succumb to addiction and/or codependency in the workplace. It doesn't matter if her feelings of inadequacy are obvious or hidden behind a veil of overachievement; the potential is there. The corporate reality is, producing more than is expected may be rewarded. This reality, when combined with the woman's deep feelings of inadequacy, paves the way for a toxic approach to work.

For instance, a woman may work long, hard hours in an

attempt to prove her worth to her father (or to those she perceives to be father figures in the workplace). Or, she may work excessively to earn the promotions, to achieve the success, that she hopes will stave off her dreadful fears of failure. Sometimes a woman's work will be noticed and rewarded, but if she is addicted to her work, it offers little comfort. Instead, it drives her to become even more successful. If a woman is codependent, she may produce sixty hours a week, month after month, perhaps year after year, and never move to a higher position or receive financial reward for her work. The end result of her extra work is that she enables the company to have a higher profit margin at her expense.

Both of these approaches are ultimately futile, for neither one can heal the wound in the daughter's heart. Whether she is addicted or codependent, the woman who has a toxic approach to work pays a terribly high price. She will pay the price in medical expenses for conditions such as ulcers, high blood pressure, and chronic headaches that result from work-related stress. She may have to pay for psychotherapy as well. She will pay the price in greater emotional distance in her relationships with her children. When a woman works sixty hours a week, goes home and tries to put the same amount of energy into home and children, there isn't anything left for her marriage, so she will pay the price there as well. If she is not married, she will pay the price in whatever long-term relationships she has, whether they be relationships with family or friends. When one considers the alternatives, it is easy to see that the inner confidence that results from the support of a loving father is a priceless gift.

Impact of the Father Wound on a Woman's Spirituality

Along with her father's emotions and attitudes toward women, a little girl seems to absorb her father's spirituality. She learns about God the Father through her relationship with her earthly father. Thus the emotional, physical, and spiritual wounds she suffers in her relationship with her father have a direct impact on her heart and soul. Those wounds leave distortions in her relationship with her heavenly Father that she will have to work out throughout the course of her life.

Ellen's father, for example, was a quiet, passive man. A good Christian, he worked hard to provide food and shelter for his family. He did not, however, build a strong emotional bridge to Ellen's heart. He was emotionally distant and seemed unaware of what his wife's depression demanded from his daughter. Her father never knew it, but Ellen grew up being a mother to her mother.

Ellen became a self-reliant woman whose view of God was distorted by her father's wounds of neglect and passivity. Sure, she believed in God. He was a nice guy, but that was about it. She didn't need to rely on Him. After all, her problems weren't so bad that she shouldn't be able to work them out on her own. God had more important people to listen to and care for than her.

Ellen surprised herself when she wrote out a description of God. When she read her description, she realized that she didn't believe God was strong enough to take care of her problems. She realized that her view of God was very similar to her view of her earthly father. Once she realized that her relationship with her heavenly Father had been dictated by her experiences with her earthly father, she began a new journey of spiritual healing.

Of course, Ellen's experience isn't the only way a daughter's heart can be opened to a deeper, more intimate experience of the heavenly Father. When a father faces his own wounds and begins to deal with his addictions or codependency, his daughter may find it easier to feel the reality of the heavenly Father in her life. As her father becomes better able to connect with his daughter on an emotional and spiritual level, she gains a greater ability to connect with her heavenly Father. An older friend of mine, named Will, had the privilege of connecting with his daughter in such a way that she was able to open her heart to the reality of her heavenly Father.

Will began his recovery when his daughter was an adult. As he realized the impact his addictions had on his daughter while she was growing up, he worked at building an emotional and spiritual bridge to her. He began expressing his feelings to her more directly. He practiced listening to her feelings without judgment or shame. In time, she felt safe in her relationship with him and had established a new level of trust in what he had to say to her.

When she was much younger, Will had tried to share the message of salvation with his daughter, but she had not accepted it. One day, on the basis of their new relationship, Will was able to introduce his daughter to her heavenly Father. This time, his daughter heard something from her father she had not been able to hear before. The reality of her relationship with her earthly father had helped her trust the reality of a relationship with her heavenly Father.

Through his response to the events of day-to-day life, every father makes a positive or negative impact on his daughter's spirituality. So it is important that he recognize the potential he has to nurture his daughter spiritually and to take advantage of the opportunities that arise. The death of my great aunt Lenora was one such opportunity I was able to share with my daughter Rachel.

Lenora was a spiritual matriarch of my family. A powerful prayer warrior, she had prayed for me every day since I was fourteen years old. Every time my family visited Minnesota, I made sure my children spent time with her. My last visit with Lenora took place in a hospital when she was ninety-five years old and in the process of dying. It was a visit I shared with Rachel.

I knew it would not be easy to visit Lenora, for she was no longer the strong, no-nonsense woman we had known and loved. Thin and weak, she was on oxygen and I.V. fluids. Yet Rachel and I went to her bedside to say goodbye. I held Lenora's hand and prayed for her. I thanked God for Lenora's life, for the way she had represented His love and grace. I thanked Him for her example of what it meant to be a strong, committed woman of God. With tears running down my face, I thanked Him for her faithfulness in praying for me and for my family for so many years. Finally, I asked Him to give her a painless journey home to be with Him.

Rachel and I walked back to our car silently. Once in the car, we cried together again and talked about how deeply Lenora had touched our lives. We talked about the tremendous legacy of spiritual commitment and strength Lenora would leave behind. I shared with Rachel how God seemed to raise up powerful women of prayer in every generation and that perhaps she would step into that role in the future.

It was not easy for me, or for Rachel, to face the reality of that day. Yet it was important that Rachel see my grief. It was important that she see how much I respected Lenora as a woman and as a woman of God. It was important that she participate in this incredible woman's last days on earth. This was part of the emotional and spiritual legacy that I, as a father, pass on to my daughter. It was one of the many ways I have to connect with my daughter and nurture her so that she can grow into her full potential as a woman of God.

Questions

1. How has contemporary culture affected the way you see yourself as a woman?

2. How has Christian culture affected the way you see yourself?

3. What "baggage" have you carried into your marriage and other relationships because of your relationship with your father?

4. In what ways has your father deepened or helped you bear those wounds?

5. What issues do you face in your workplace because of your relationship with your father?

CHAPTER 4

Building Healthy Boundaries

A father plays a crucial role in nurturing the development of his daughter's boundaries.

Following King Xerxes' proclamation, many young women were brought into the citadel of Susa to be prepared to enter the king's harem. Hegai, the king's eunuch who was responsible for the harem, was very impressed by Esther. He saw to it that she received the best food, the finest beauty treatments, and placed her in the most luxurious accommodations in the harem. He even hand picked seven maids from the king's palace to serve her. And so Esther embarked on a full year of preparation before she would be taken to the king.

The preparation was the same for all the young women. Twelve months of beauty treatments began with six months of treatment with oil of myrrh followed by six months of treatment with perfumes and cosmetics. When each young woman's time of preparation was complete, she would be taken into the king's palace in the evening. She would be given anything she wanted to take to the palace. The next morning she would be returned to the part of the harem that was reserved for the king's concubines. She would not see the king again unless he requested her by name.

During her time of preparation, Esther impressed everyone who saw her. When it was her time to be taken to the king, Esther asked Hegai what she should take to the palace with her. She followed his instructions exactly. The king, too, was impressed with Esther. "She won his favor and approval more than any of the other virgins. So he set a royal crown on her head and made her queen instead of Vashti."

What a celebration followed! King Xerxes was so pleased with his new queen that he proclaimed a royal holiday throughout his empire. In Esther's honor, he gave generous gifts and conducted a great banquet for all of his noblemen. Despite her new status in the spotlight of the Persian Empire, Esther "kept secret her family background and nationality just as Mordecai had told her to do, for she continued to follow Mordecai's instructions as she had done when he was bringing her up."[1]

Wow! Esther had it made. Can you imagine what it was like for her, a captive Jewish orphan, to be catapulted into this lifestyle? She had all the trappings of the rich and famous and didn't even have to win the lottery to do it! It was as if she lived in a luxurious beauty spa. She was fed the world's best foods, given the most exotic beauty treatments, and adorned with the finest cosmetics. Life in the Persian Empire didn't get better than this.

To live in the king's harem was to participate in an environment and lifestyle that could sweep a young woman off her feet. It would have been easy for Esther (or any young woman) to become totally absorbed in her new life and forget the training she had received at home. It would have been easy for her personal boundaries to collapse under the pressure of conforming to such a high standard of external beauty. It would have been easy for her to lose her identity amid the whirlwind of royal life. But these things did not happen to Esther. Despite the distractions surrounding her, she continued to maintain her boundaries and follow Mordecai's instructions.

I do not believe it is an accident that Esther was able to stand strong in her new role as King Xerxes' queen. I believe it was a natural outcome of the relationship that existed between Esther and Mordecai. Mordecai had both loved and trained his daughter well. As such, she had solid, strong boundaries that enabled her to thrive in the midst of unpredictable and potentially risky circumstances. Like Esther, daughters today need strong, solid boundaries if they are to survive in an unpredictable and risky world. Thus today's fathers need to nurture their daughters' boundaries by providing the kind of love and training that Mordecai gave to Esther.

What Are Boundaries?

Boundaries are essential to ensure the inner safety of every human being. They comprise all the beliefs and feelings that serve as barriers to anything that might harm a person. They are like invisible fences that provide spiritual, emotional, and physical protection.

One way to illustrate how boundaries work is to imagine a medieval castle that is surrounded by a tall, strong wall. The wall provides protection from enemies. Within the walls, the life of the castle community is safe. Families live in safety. People conduct their business in the castle courtyard without fear of attack. Children have a safe place to run, skip, jump, and play games. In addition, sentries on top of the walls watch what happens inside and outside the castle. They question those who want to come inside the castle walls to conduct business and deny admittance to anyone who would bring harm. The presence of the wall and the watchful sentries are a formidable obstacle to any attack.

So it is with a person's boundaries. Boundaries set a safe atmosphere that enables us to learn how to survive and live in an unsafe world. They enable us to know when we are at risk and give us the ability to take steps to protect ourselves. They help us define areas of personal responsibility and enable us to refuse to carry responsibilities that rightfully belong to others. Boundaries keep toxic feelings and information out and allow healing to occur when we have been wounded by the world. In short, boundaries help us develop and live out the full potential God has intended for us.

Although we may not always be aware of them, boundaries play an essential role in the physical, emotional, and spiritual areas of life. All of us are keenly aware of the boundary of our visible, physical bodies, but we are usually less aware of our invisible boundaries. Even though we can't see the invisible boundaries, we can certainly feel them. The following exercise will help you feel an invisible physical boundary.

Stand up and ask a friend or family member to walk toward you. As the person approaches you, you will at some point begin to feel uncomfortable. That point of discomfort represents your invisible physical boundary with that person. The boundary may be anywhere from a few inches to several feet away from you. If your boundaries are severely damaged, it is possible that you will begin to feel uncomfortable while the person is still on the other side of the room or, on the other extreme, you may allow the person to walk right into you!

We also have emotional and spiritual boundaries that are just as real as our physical boundaries. Often feelings of fear, anger, or shame are the points of discomfort that indicate when a spiritual or emotional boundary is being crossed. If our boundaries are damaged, we may be too afraid or otherwise unable to stand up for ourselves and express our feelings when another person is angry or abusive toward us. If our boundaries are intact, however, we will be able to take a stand for ourselves in such situations.

What Is a Father's Role in Nurturing Boundaries?

God created us in such a way that we need physical, emotional, and spiritual boundaries. They are an essential part of our humanity. But no one is born with boundaries; they are something we must learn. We learn about boundaries very early in life, primarily through our interaction with our parents and secondarily through our relationships with our extended family. Both parents play a significant role in helping a daughter build the boundaries she needs to live successfully in this world. In fact, helping children establish appropriate, protective boundaries is one of the most important tasks for parents to accomplish.

During infancy parents provide complete protection and safety for their children, but parents cannot do that forever. Therefore parents must teach their children how to set their own boundaries so they will continue to be protected throughout life. Some of the boundaries parents must help their children establish include:

- Setting firm limits and intervening if the children move into something that is harmful or potentially destructive. (This type of boundary setting is especially important during adolescence and is often greeted with unhappiness.)
- Stepping in to stop shaming or abusive behavior that others (including extended family members) may inflict.
- Respecting their children's need for privacy and modesty.
- Protecting their children from pornography and other inappropriate sexual messages that may appear on television or in books and magazines.
- Respecting the manner in which their children connect with God.
- Helping children learn what their appropriate responsibilities are (and are not) in various relationships.
- Defining appropriate behavior in different situations.
- Teaching children that no one needs to touch their bodies or private areas, and that it is okay to say "no" when physical closeness makes them feel uncomfortable.

By modeling good boundaries, by actively teaching about boundaries, and by being emotionally involved in a daughter's life, both the mother and father empower a daughter. They empower her with an understanding of the world around her and a sense of confidence in her unique identity that enables her to make her way in the world. Most of us recognize that the mother plays a significant role in this process, however, the father's role in this process is generally underestimated. The daughter whose boundaries are nurtured by *both* the mother and father is fortunate indeed. The mother can model or instruct about a particular boundary, but it also helps when the father conveys the same message. The father's input has a rock-solid quality that is invaluable. When a daughter has an emotional and spiritual connection with both of her parents and receives teaching from both of them, she does not stand alone; she stands on very solid ground.

I think Esther received this kind of love and training from Mordecai. He strongly affirmed Esther's value and identity. He also taught her about some of the boundaries she would need to set if she were to survive in the world in which they lived. He let her know that there were dangerous people in the world and that she dare not consider the world to be a safe place. He taught her that she must protect herself by keeping her precious identity to herself and watching out for those who would harm her. There is no substitute for this kind of love and nurturing from a father.

When a father maintains good boundaries with his daughter and is able to express his love for her in a caring way and respect her for who she is, he has gone a long way toward helping her survive in the world. He has done much to ensure that she will have safe relationships with her peers, teachers, pastors, physicians, and authority figures of all types. Through her relationship with her father, she gains a guideline or model of what appropriate, safe behavior is. Without his nurturing, she is at great risk.

Through family relationships, particularly her relationship with her father, a daughter discovers what it means to establish boundaries in the ups and downs of daily life. What she learns through these family relationships sets the course for much of her adult relationships. When her parents set spiritual, emotional, and physical boundaries, a daughter is safe and has the opportunity to learn, express creativity, and grow. When they are affirming, nurturing, and respectful of her and her boundaries, she grows up with an ability to identify and hold onto who she is as a person. She has a healthy self-confidence. She is able to express her feelings directly and is able to set boundaries in her relationships with others. But if her boundaries are violated or damaged during early childhood, those boundaries will fail her later in life.

The Problem With Boundaries

All too often a child's boundaries are violated. When boundary violations occur, setting boundaries becomes a problem. The difficulty in setting boundaries may occur in adolescence and will often continue well into adult life.

Boundary violations are any experiences, events, or patterns that wound a child. Although boundary violations come in innumerable forms, some of the more common ones include, but are not limited to:

- Raging at a child.
- Ignoring or scorning a child's feelings.
- Touching a child sexually, making inappropriate sexual comments, or viewing pornography with a child.
- Turning to the child, rather than to the spouse, for emotional support.
- Physically abusing a child, which includes excessive physical punishment.

In reality, a boundary violation is an experience of abuse for the inner child. It wounds her very soul. It lowers her self-esteem and leaves her with feelings of shame, anxiety, and fear.

Every boundary violation becomes a learning experience for the child that will stick with her throughout life, impacting every area of life. When a child's boundaries are violated, she learns that the world is a scary place. She receives a very confusing message and fails to learn how or where to set appropriate boundaries. She loses confidence in her identity and her ability to express her needs and desires, which leads to boundary failure later in life.

Sadly, many of these boundary violations come at the hand of parents, fathers, grandfathers, teachers, church leaders, and other authority figures whose job it is to nurture—not destroy—a young girl's boundaries. The violations may be as subtle as a shaming look or a glance of disapproval, or as violent as a beating or forced sexual activity. No matter how the violation occurs or how seemingly insignificant it may appear to be, the result is always the same: the child is traumatized. Even if a child is unaware that a boundary is supposed to exist, she feels a wound deep inside when it is violated. That wound impacts every aspect of her being. To better understand what it means to nurture boundaries and to see how easily boundaries are violated, we will now consider some of the most common areas in which boundary violations occur.

Nurturing Relationships vs. Covert Incest

God designed the family to operate in such a way that the primary relationship exists between the husband and wife. But in a troubled marriage, this often does not happen. When the spiritual and emotional bond between husband and wife is weak or broken, the primary relationship often exists between child and parent rather than between husband and wife. This is called *covert incest*. Covert incest, which is perhaps the most common form of emotional and sexual abuse today, shatters the child's boundaries. Kenneth Adams aptly describes the devastating impact of covert incest:

> *Covert incest* occurs when a child becomes the object of a parent's affection, love, passion and preoccupation. The par-

ent, motivated by the loneliness and emptiness created by a chronically troubled marriage or relationship, makes the child a surrogate partner. The boundary between caring and incestuous love is crossed when the relationship with the child exists to meet the needs of the parent rather than those of the child. As the deterioration in the marriage progresses, the dependency on the child grows and the opposite-sex parent's response to the child becomes increasingly characterized by desperation, jealousy, and a disregard for personal boundaries. The child becomes an object to be manipulated and used so the parent can avoid the pain and reality of a troubled marriage.

The child feels used and trapped, the same feelings overt incest victims experience. Attempts at play, autonomy, and friendship render the child guilt-ridden and lonely, never able to feel okay about his or her needs. Over time, the child

---

Symptoms of Covert Incest

The symptoms of covert incest are not difficult to recognize. Most of them apply to adult children as well as to younger children:

- The parent looks toward the child for emotional support that is not provided by the spouse.

- The child is the primary source of the parent's emotional support.

- The parent would rather spend time with the child than with the spouse.

- The parent shares angry, critical feelings with the child concerning the spouse.

- The parent's happiness rises and falls with the child's accomplishments.

---

becomes preoccupied with the parent's needs and feels protective and concerned. A psychological marriage between parent and child results. The child becomes the parent's surrogate spouse.

. . . An important difference between overt and covert incest is that, while the overt victim feels abused, the covert victim feels idealized and privileged. Yet underneath the thin mask of feeling special and privileged rests the same trauma of the overt victim: rage anger, shame and guilt. . . . The adult covert incest victim remains stuck in a pattern of living aimed at keeping the special relationships going with the opposite-sex parent. It is a pattern of always trying to please Mommy or Daddy.[2]

When covert incest is at work, a part of the daughter's childhood comes to an end. She is forced, prematurely, out

- The parent becomes resentful or jealous of the child's happiness or accomplishments.

- The child is afraid or worried that the parent's marriage will fail unless he or she supports the parent(s).

- The child worries about what might happen if he or she isn't available to meet the parent's needs.

- The married child is closer and more emotionally supportive of his or her parent than his or her spouse.

- The child feels that he or she exists to meet the parent's needs, but since the parent does not reciprocate, the child feels used or manipulated.

- The parent provides emotional support and encouragement for the child, but doesn't provide such support for the spouse.

of the world of a child and into the world of an adult. Her boundaries are not nurtured, and she begins to live life through the eyes of her parent.

Sue, for example, remembers being like a wife to her father since she was six years old. Her family had a high profile in the church, but they hid a dreadful secret: Sue's mother was an alcoholic. Ever since she can remember, Sue's father depended on her to keep up the family image. He would tell her what she needed to do and would praise her for her help. Whenever they could, Sue and her father did special things together. While they were off having a good time, he would talk to Sue about how lonely he was and what a lousy mother she had. Sue's mother became increasingly resentful of the relationship her husband and daughter shared.

By the time Sue reached adolescence, her mother's rage was out of control—partially due to the progression of her disease and partially due to what was happening in the relationship between her daughter and husband. For years Sue's father had been treating Sue as if she were his wife, and as she developed into a young woman her father's touch became sexual rather than paternal. Whenever he hugged Sue, he found a way to brush his hand against her breast. He would even do this in her mother's presence, which usually triggered her mother's angry attack on Sue— an attack Sue's father did nothing to stop.

As soon as she could, Sue left home and married. But she wasn't happy in her marriage. In fact, much of her energy was consumed by the anger and resentment she felt toward her passive husband. In Sue's eyes, her husband never did anything. (And she was close to being right!) Sue was the one who handled the family finances. She was the one who began and conducted any discussion of family problems. She was the one who made the decision to go out to eat.

She was the one who initiated sex. In many ways, Sue had married her father. She had married a man who needed her to take care of him just as her father had needed her.

Of course, this is not the only way covert incest occurs. Emotional incest occurs between mothers and daughters as well. Deb, for example, was the daughter of a traveling salesman. Her mother had always struggled with depression. Ever since Deb could remember, her mother had gone into a rage or thrown a tantrum when she didn't get her way. Sometimes her depression had been so deep that she stayed in bed for days.

By the time Deb reached her early teens, her mother had become incapable of managing the household. One day her father took her aside and said, "We have to be really careful of your mother now. She isn't doing well. She is really fragile. I need you to take care of her." Deb did as she was told. She took care of her mother and her younger brothers and sisters. *Mom is sick,* she thought. *Dad wants me to take care of her. He will be really happy with me if I do a good job. God will be pleased with me, too, because I honor my parents when I take care of my mother.*

This was such a compelling message for Deb that she was still taking care of her mother thirty years later! It wasn't until Deb was in her mid-forties that she realized her father had abdicated his responsibility to care for his wife and given it to his daughter. She also realized, with a crushing sadness, that she could do nothing to obtain her father's love, no matter how much she cared for her mother. This was a difficult wound for Deb to bear.

It is one thing to help out and take care of a parent when there is illness or a crisis in the family, but parents need to make sure the household returns to normal as soon as possible. In this case, Deb's father took away her childhood by giving her the responsibility to care for her mother. He elevated Deb to a special status in the family, but it was not for her benefit. It was for his and his wife's benefit, which violated Deb's boundaries.

Covert incest may occur in other ways as well. In families where the father is absent, emotionally detached, or involved in an addiction, the mother-daughter relationship may become too close. In this kind of situation the mother and daughter may share everything, with the result that the daughter loses her childhood by becoming an equal with her mother. This is particularly risky if the marriage is experiencing difficulty. It is then all too easy for the mother to share her hurts about the marriage with her daughter. A child should *never* be put in the position of taking on the troubles of a marriage. This is a terrible violation of the child's boundaries. Marriages will always have some trouble, but it is the parents' responsibility to set the boundaries and seek the support they need from God and from others so that children aren't required to bear the hurts of their parents.

The essential thing to remember is that God intended parents to be available to meet the needs of their children. When covert incest occurs, the roles are switched. The parents no longer exist to meet the children's needs; the children exist to meet the parents' needs. That is a devastating boundary violation.

We see a beautiful illustration of appropriate parent-child boundaries in Esther's story: "Every day he [Mordecai] walked back and forth near the courtyard of the harem to find out how Esther was and what was happening to her."[3] Mordecai was there for his daughter every day! He was not there for his own benefit, to see what he could gain by hanging out with the rich and famous. He was there to meet Esther's needs. He was concerned about her welfare and wanted to make sure she was safe. That is the kind of nurturing relationship that God intends for fathers and daughters.

Addiction vs. Availability

If a father is to meet his daughter's needs as God intended, he must be emotionally available to her. But when a father turns to an addiction to numb his pain, he deadens himself to the feelings of his children. It simply is not possible to be addicted and emotionally available at the same time. So an addicted father cannot feel or even desire to respond to the needs of his daughter's heart. It doesn't matter what addiction a father practices—work, sex, eating, drugs, whatever—it will wound his daughter.

Addiction leaves chronic tension and fear in its wake. As the father's addiction progresses, that tension and fear can turn into terror. Many adult daughters of alcoholic fathers still remember the jolt of fear they felt whenever they heard the father come into the house. They never knew whether he would be sober or drunk, irritable or raging. Some still remember the shock and confusion they felt when they walked into the family room late one night and saw him watching a pornographic movie and masturbating. Some still fear asking the father for anything because they remember all too well how many times he came home from work and irritably shouted "No!" when asked to fix a bike or to play. Others still feel terrified at night, fearful that he might soon be next to the bed, touching or raping. Some cringe at the sound of raised voices, because they remember the scary nights when mom and dad would fight, and he would storm out of the house to seek solace at the office, with his lover, or in a bar. Still other daughters of legalistic, perfectionistic fathers seek the narrow way to the father's heart—a route that only an anorexic or bulimic daughter could walk.

All of these wounds, and many more, come from fathers who are not emotionally available to their daughters. All of these wounds leave a daughter with a damaged boundary system. Since the father is the first man a daughter learns to love, she naturally desires to be emotionally close to him— whether he is capable of providing that closeness or not. Unfortunately, the daughter of an addicted father learns by experience that men will be emotionally unavailable and unresponsive. This lesson follows her throughout life, leading her to feel most comfortable when she is in relationship with addicted men.

Rage vs. Safety

Parental rage is a horrible experience for a child to endure. It naturally sets off an uncontrollable fear response in the child. The adrenal glands start producing adrenaline that triggers a natural "fight or flight" response. Since small children learn quickly that they cannot fight back, they are left in an incredible state of fear, the symptoms of which are physically evident in their bodies. Children can learn to live with the chronic tension of fear, but later in life they often pay a high price in terms of panic attacks, chronic headaches, colon problems, and a host of other stress-induced diseases.

Rather than nurturing a daughter to develop her potential as the unique creation God intended her to be, a raging father squelches his daughter's uniqueness and feeds her development as a codependent. A little girl who is raged at learns to walk very carefully, always pleasing others. Self-denial, which for some Christian women is a comfortable theology, becomes a way of life.

The daughter of a raging father is emotionally set up to have an unhappy marriage. She may go to one extreme and marry a controlling, abusive man. Or she may go to the opposite extreme and marry a man who is so "safe" that he is benign. He may be so passive that she needs to give him a Geritol® I.V. just to make sure he is still alive! By the time she reaches age forty, she may be tempted to take her husband into an electro-convulsive therapy unit to see if anything can jump start him into activity.

It is easy to point the finger of blame at a raging father, but the blame doesn't stop there. It is also true that a passive, codependent mother wounds her daughter when she is unwilling or unable to stop the father's rage. The mother's passivity reinforces the damage done by the father's rage. By doing nothing to protect her daughter, the passive mother communicates that it is normal to be abused and that rage is a natural part of a relationship with a man.

It is important that we don't overlook the fact that rage from the mother is just as devastating to a little girl as rage from the father. When a daughter suffers rage from her mother, her feminine self-concept is distorted. The daughter learns to handle anger in the same destructive way her mother does, or she learns to deny her anger and pretend it doesn't exist. If she takes this latter course, any anger she has brings on feelings of shame and fear, even if her anger is normal or justified. She may fear that her anger will explode uncontrollably, just like her mother's rage, so she may never learn how to measure or restrain her anger. She develops no middle ground, only the extremes of rage or no response at all.

Many women have suffered deep wounds because their fathers did not put a stop to their mothers' rage. When a father does not take active steps to stop the abuse of a mother's rage, his lack of action in effect sanctions the abuse. Jennifer, for example, grew up with a raging mother and a codependent father. Her father was an effective minister in a growing church. Outside the home, the family was the perfect image of a peaceful, loving family; behind closed doors, the mother ruled with rage.

Now an adult, Jennifer views God as a passive, ineffective force. She believes that everything that happens in her life rests on her shoulders alone. She still goes to church, but her heart isn't in it. In fact, her heart isn't in much of anything because she learned to turn off the feelings of her heart in order to survive her mother's rage. Although her father was a nice, loving man who had no intention of harming his daughter, his passivity in the face of his wife's rage greatly wounded his daughter. That wound is played out daily in his daughter's adult life.

Sexual Abuse vs. Physical Closeness

God has placed in each of us a need to be loved, comforted, and nurtured by a mother and a father. When a father holds his little girl, he meets a spiritual, emotional, and physical need deep within her. That physical closeness helps give the daughter a sense of value and confidence in who she is. A natural outgrowth of a solid, valuable, personal identity is the ability to set boundaries. Thus her father's physical touch greatly influences a daughter's boundaries. His touch either strengthens or wounds her boundaries.

Of all the ways a father can wound his daughter, the impact of his touch through sexual abuse is one of the most devastating. Sexual abuse is a boundary violation that destroys the soul. It literally separates the inner person. To survive this kind of violation, the little girl dissociates or detaches from the situation and the feelings that accompany it. Once she disassociates from her feelings in an effort to survive, she continues to have difficulty recognizing and responding to her feelings throughout life.

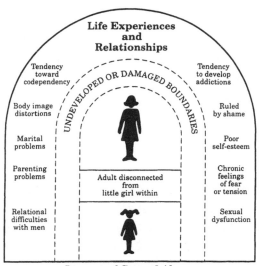

Impact of Sexual Abuse
on Adult Woman's Life

Sexual abuse is far more widespread than most of us realize. We easily recognize that rape is sexual abuse, but there are more subtle forms of sexual abuse as well. Consider the following behaviors that some fathers practice:

- Denigrating treatment of women, including verbal comments about women's bodies and forms of visual commentary such as staring at a woman's breasts.
- Sexual addiction, which may include viewing pornography, involvement in prostitution, asking the daughter to wear certain types of clothing, and/or participation in extramarital affairs.
- Touching or fondling various body parts or inappropriate kissing.
- Failing to respect the daughter's boundaries and need for privacy by walking into the bathroom or bedroom when the daughter is getting dressed or by bathing with the daughter.

- Treating the mother as a sexual object rather than a person.
- Making comments about the daughter's body or sexuality, such as commenting about the size of her breasts.
- Telling sexual jokes.
- Talking to his daughter about his sexual relationship with his wife or other women.
- Adhering to any ideology or theology that shames or dominates women.

All of these forms of sexual abuse are devastating to a girl. They leave her with a shattered sense of self, distorted body image, damaged sexuality, inappropriate (or nonexistent) boundaries, memory gaps, post-traumatic stress syndrome, difficulty in interpersonal relationships, and fertile ground for the growth of codependency and addictions. They send mixed messages to a daughter and confuse the lines between closeness, affection, and sex itself.

Although abuse by the father is particularly devastating to a daughter, we must recognize that fathers are not the only important men in a little girl's life. Grandfathers, uncles, family friends, pastors, teachers, doctors, therapists, and others also function as father figures in a girl's life. In the girl's eyes, all male authority figures carry the impact of her father. So sexual abuse by any of the men listed above is wounding to a daughter.

It is no secret that one out of every four women will experience sexual assault during her lifetime. This is why a father who wants to nurture his daughter needs to actively take steps to strengthen her personal boundaries and to protect her from sexual abuse. He does this first by honoring her boundaries himself. As she grows up, he respects her need for privacy, makes sure that he hugs and kisses her appropriately, and models appropriate boundaries with other women.

With a basis of good boundaries in his relationship with his daughter, a father can then teach her that she has control over her body. From the age of three or four, his daughter needs to know that there is a difference between good touch and bad touch. As she grows older, he strengthens those boundaries by teaching her that she has a right to say "no" to any touch or hug that makes her feel uncomfortable. He teaches her that if anyone touches her in a bad way—whether it be grandpa, the neighbor, a teacher, or a pastor—it is okay for her to run away, scream, or tell the whole world what happened. He affirms that there are no secrets, that she is not responsible to protect any other person.

The father's role in respecting and strengthening his daughter's sexual boundaries is of utmost significance. All sexual boundary violations leave deep wounds that have life-long consequences. They leave an adult woman who faces abusive men feeling as helpless as she was when she was abused as a little girl. They rob a woman of her ability to set the protective boundaries that an adult woman should be able to set. They strip her of the strength to stand against abusive treatment and bring it to the attention of others who can share her pain and support her.

There is no way to overestimate the impact a father's sexual abuse has on his daughter. One sexual comment damages his daughter's boundaries. One inappropriate touch tears her soul. These wounds are felt deeply in her body, soul, and emotions. If she suffers these wounds, it takes a tremendous amount of work on her part to recover.

Disrespectful vs. Respectful Attitudes Toward Feminine

In addition to needing strong boundaries that provide sexual protection, women need strong boundaries just to withstand the onslaught of disrespectful and demeaning attitudes that women face. As Queen Vashti learned many years ago, a woman must be able to take steps to protect herself if she lives in a world in which women are viewed as second-class citizens. As is true in other boundary issues, the father's attitude and actions toward women either wound his daughter or strengthen her.

There are many ways in which a father can nurture his daughter's personal boundaries and feminine identity. When he respects women in general and treats his wife as a valuable partner in his life, he affirms that women have value. When he honors his daughter's intuition and values her feminine qualities, he lays a solid groundwork on which she can develop a healthy pride in her feminine identity. When he considers her feelings, opinions, and perspectives to be valuable and important, he strengthens her self-confidence. When he encourages her to explore and develop the potential God has given her, she is better able to pursue her dreams. When a father develops this kind of foundational relationship with his daughter, he is then able to teach her a great deal about how to survive in a world where not everyone views her as valuable.

What is sad is that many men do not respect or value women. They view women as second-class citizens. They are threatened by women of strength. They feel nothing for the heart of a woman; they merely see her as a sex object. Men who view women in this way violate a woman's boundaries. When a girl is unfortunate enough to be the daughter of such a man, she is wounded deeply in her soul. She grows up with a damaged view of herself and her feminine nature that sets her up for relationships with men that are characterized by abuse, codependency, or anger.

Every woman will run into some men who are disrespectful of women. A daughter is much better prepared to deal with these men if her father has honored her feminine character through his relationship with her and also instructed her in how to set boundaries that protect her value. When a father and daughter have an emotionally connected relationship, the daughter most likely will come to him with questions or be open to talking about what is happening in her life.

For example, she may talk to her father about a teacher who is mistreating her at school. At these times the father can listen to his daughter. If she is up against a shaming teacher, the father can validate her reality. He can affirm that she doesn't need to fear authority figures, that authority figures are to treat her with respect and understanding. He can help her learn that an authority figure who is domineering or disrespectful has a problem and that she needs to have strong boundaries with that kind of person. If his daughter is not yet mature enough to set those boundaries herself, he can take appropriate action to set those boundaries for her.

The father who cares about his daughter's safety in the world will also anticipate the risks she will face and prepare her to navigate through those difficult areas. Mordecai did this for Esther by teaching her that it was not safe to reveal her Jewish background. Fathers today do this by teaching their daughters that some men do not respect women and that she has the right to set boundaries with those men.

"Do not expect men to have boundaries," one father taught his daughter. "No man has the right to talk to you or touch you in a way that is not respectful. When you are in junior high school and boys try to pinch you or pull on your bra, they are violating your boundaries. They are not treating you with respect. You can tell them to stop it. If they persist, you can go ahead and kick them!"

It isn't easy for daughters to stand up to the disrespect for women that is so prevalent in our culture. One day, for example, our family walked across a restaurant parking lot. I was walking with my wife and our two youngest daughters. Our older children, Ben and Rachel, walked some distance behind us. As we walked, a pickup truck with several guys in the back passed between us. They whistled and shouted something at Rachel. I didn't hear what they said, but I did see the look on my daughter's face.

When we had a minute to ourselves I said, "Rachel, you looked really confused when that pickup truck went by in the parking lot. Was it something they said to you?" She nodded. I looked her in the eye and continued. "You are not what those men think you are. Their whistling and comments is their stuff, not yours. How they view you has nothing to do with who you are. You are Rachel. Nothing those men say can change that."

A father's respect for his daughter and who she is does much to strengthen her in the face of a destructive world. When a father builds up his daughter's boundaries by the way he loves her and what he teaches her, he empowers her to live out the potential God has given her. Such a father is truly a blessing to his daughter.

Questions

1. How has your father helped you draw appropriate boundary lines?

2. How do you wish your father had been better able to help you establish your boundaries?

3. Has your father ever violated your boundaries? How?

4. Do you feel safe with and respected by your father?

5. Evaluate the condition of your boundaries.

CHAPTER 5

Living in the Real World

A father plays a crucial role in enabling his daughter to face the difficult realities of life.

To look at her, one would think that Esther was the luckiest woman in the whole Persian Empire. She had the best life had to offer—riches, servants, beautiful clothes, prestige, and a king for a husband. Still, the Persian Empire was a dangerous place in which to live, even for the queen. And Esther's father, Mordecai, was well aware of the dangers.

When Esther became queen, Mordecai did not abandon her to her new life and merrily pursue his own interests. Instead, he remained as close to her as possible and sat every day at the king's gate—listening, watching, and waiting for news of Esther. One day, during the course of his daily vigil, he discovered that two of the king's guards planned to assassinate King Xerxes! Immediately Mordecai informed Esther of the plot. Esther then warned the king of the danger and told him that Mordecai had uncovered the conspiracy. When the king investigated the report, he found it to be true and had the offending guards hanged. The king's life was spared, and the entire story was written in the official record of the king's reign.

However, the king's guards were not the only men in the Persian Empire who aspired to improve their status and would use any means possible to achieve their goal. There was also a nobleman by the name of Haman whose desire for honor knew no bounds. He was already the most highly honored nobleman, for King Xerxes had commanded the royal officials at the king's gate to kneel before him. All of the officials obeyed except one Jew, Mordecai.

Apparently, the other royal officials didn't like the idea that they knelt down before Haman but Mordecai did not. Day after day, they asked Mordecai why he did not obey the king's command. He simply told them that he was a Jew and that he would not bow before Haman. When they realized that no amount of persuasion would cause Mordecai to do otherwise, they went to Haman to see if he would tolerate Mordecai's behavior. As one might expect, he did not. In fact, he became so enraged that he wanted to destroy not only Mordecai but every Jew in the Persian Empire!

When his evil plan was ready, Haman went to King Xerxes. "There is a certain people dispersed and scattered among the peoples in all the provinces of your kingdom," he said, "whose customs are different from those of all other people and who do not obey the king's laws; it is not in the king's best interest to tolerate them." Haman then proposed a bargain with the king. If the king would issue a decree to destroy those people, Haman would donate 345 *metric tons of silver to the king's treasury to pay off the soldiers to do the job.*

The king was easily persuaded. He told Haman to do whatever he wanted to with the people and told him to keep the money also! Soon the order to destroy the Jews went out from one end of the empire to the other.

While King Xerxes and Haman celebrated the decree by drinking together, the Jews went into mourning. In every province they fasted, wept, and wailed. Many of them lay in sackcloth and ashes. As soon as Mordecai heard the news, "he tore his clothes, put on sackcloth and ashes, and went out into the city wailing loudly and bitterly." He was not allowed to pass through the king's gate because he was mourning, so he sat down in the open square in front of the king's gate.[1]

Who would have guessed that such dangers lurked in the midst of such a mighty empire! No wonder Mordecai told Esther to keep her ethnic origin to herself. It is a good thing she followed his instructions and told no one—not even her husband—that she was a Jew. Even the queen had to face the reality of life-threatening challenges. How fortunate she was to have received the blessing of her father's understanding love and wise training while she was growing up.

The Blessing of a Strong, Wise, and Feeling Father

In this part of Esther's story, we learn a bit more about who Mordecai is. We discover previously unknown aspects of his character. We gain insight into his fathering. We gain a glimpse of the strength of his convictions. Let's look more closely at the man who fathered Esther.

Mordecai was apparently wise. Since he sat at the king's

gate among the royal officials, it is possible that he was an elder in the city. Others probably came to him for advice or to resolve disputes. But we also know Mordecai had another reason for being at the king's gate: to look out for Esther's best interests. He wanted to be as close to her as possible so that he could hear how she was doing and so that she could send messages to him if needed. He wanted to do as much as possible to keep her safe.

As circumstances turned out, Mordecai was in the right place at the right time. When he learned of the plot to kill King Xerxes, he took immediate action and warned Esther. Their quick action saved the day. If Xerxes had been killed, Esther would have been in a very precarious position. Chances are she would have been killed, or at the least enslaved, by whoever strong-armed his way into power. By saving the king's life Mordecai also saved Esther.

Mordecai was not only wise, but was a man of integrity and courage. He was not afraid to take the risk and stand up for what he believed. Even when pressured by his peers, Mordecai didn't give in. He was not afraid to say that he was a Jew and would bow to worship no one but Jehovah. His action left no doubt about the value he placed on his religious beliefs.

What a contrast we see between Mordecai and Haman! Whereas Mordecai stands out as a man of principle, Haman stands out as a man who grasps for whatever pleases him. Honor bestowed on Haman went straight to his arrogant head. When he felt that he had been crossed, he was determined to destroy not only his enemy but everything his enemy held dear. Haman was so obsessed with causing Mordecai pain that he would give up great riches, if necessary, to carry out his evil plan. Haman's hate was so powerful that he sent out an edict to kill an entire race of people —old women, innocent babies, playful children, working men, and young mothers—and to plunder everything they owned. His heart was so evil that he sat down and enjoyed a drink after his plan was approved.

Faced with men like this, it is no wonder that Mordecai instructed Esther as he did. He knew the history of his people and how quickly situations could change that would endanger their entire race. He may well have known from experience that in the Persian Empire the anger of one powerful man could lead to the death of many. He may well have suspected that there was an undercurrent of anti-Semitism among the king and his officials.

As these frightening events unfold, we see tangible evidence of the great well of emotional and spiritual feeling that springs up from the depths of Mordecai's soul. When he learned the dreadful news of what was to befall his people, his whole being responded in pain. His normal life came to a screeching halt. He cried out, he tore his clothes, he put on clothes of mourning, and he publicly proclaimed the atrocity of what had been decreed.

Through his actions, Mordecai assumed a place of spiritual and community leadership. He didn't take one look at the edict and take off to save his own skin. He didn't organize a mass exodus. Instead, he went straight to the king's gate. There we see him pleading before God, in full view of the king, for the great loss of innocent lives that has been decreed. God's Word encourages His people to bring before Him the anguish of our hearts: "Put on sackcloth, O priests, and mourn; wail, you who minister before the altar. Come, spend the night in sackcloth, you who minister before my God. . . ."[2] In the face of such grave circumstances, this is exactly what Mordecai did.

This is something fathers today can and need to do as well. Bob, for example, learned that his daughter had been sexually abused by a man in his church. Devastated, he went to the church leaders to seek a biblical response to this violation of his daughter. To his dismay, the church leaders refused to take action and went on as if nothing had happened. Bob could not accept their denial of the great wound inflicted on his daughter. He next reported the abuse to the police so that the legal system would recognize the damage done and hold the perpetrator accountable. In taking this step, Bob set aside any concern for his standing in the eyes of the church leaders. He chose instead to affirm that his daughter's pain was real and important, to communicate that she was too valuable to be treated abusively, and to ensure the future safety of other little girls in the church. This is the kind of father who will have a tremendous impact on his daughter's life.

It isn't difficult to imagine what a positive influence Mordecai was on Esther. Throughout her life, he touched her heart in such a way that she was open and eager for his instruction. He not only taught her what it meant to live with personal integrity in society, he modeled it. Likewise, a father today who develops this kind of relationship with his daughter gives her much. But there is more. A father can also play an important role in helping his daughter deal with the world as it really is. It is in this area that Mordecai truly shines.

Exposing the Fantasy

I think all of us—men as well as women—want to believe that life will be fair, that if we work hard we will be justly rewarded, that if we treat others well they will treat us well, and that others can be trusted to respect and protect us. It is unfortunate, but this is not real life. Life isn't that way today, and it wasn't that way when Esther and Mordecai lived. In light of this harsh reality, a father plays an extremely important role in breaking through the comfortable myths in which daughters (and sons) are tempted to seek refuge.

Robert Bly, the noted storyteller and poet who has sparked a men's movement, tells a story about a father who encourages his little girl to jump off the front steps into his arms. She is afraid to do it, but he convinces her that she won't get hurt because he will catch her. So she timidly jumps off the steps and lands safely in his arms. Then he tells her to do it again. She does, and he catches her. The third time, she eagerly climbs the steps and fearlessly jumps toward him. This time he does not catch her. She falls to the ground and looks up at her father. "The world is not your mother!" he says.

Obviously this father's methods need a strong dose of compassion, but there is certainly truth in his message. It is easy for a daughter to think that *the world is my mother*, that it is a better place than it actually is. So her father presents a great gift to her if he is available and willing to ground her solidly in reality. As we saw in the previous chapter, the process of teaching a daughter to deal with life as it is, rather than as she would like it to be, begins when the father nurtures the development of his daughter's boundaries. This process continues as the daughter matures and operates increasingly in the world outside the home.

The loving, feeling father will not be afraid to confront his daughter with life as it really is. When, even as a preschooler, she runs headlong into her first lessons that life is not fair, her father can help her face that reality. He can help open her eyes to the truth, even if it isn't very pretty. He can help her grieve the painful loss of innocence that comes with knowledge. He can help her discern between her responsibilities and the responsibilities of others. He can help her cope with the good as well as the bad in life.

This is a role the father plays, although to an increasingly lesser extent, throughout his daughter's life. If he does his job well, his adult daughter will be well equipped to deal with life in the real world. Most of the time, she will handle life confidently without his counsel and assistance. But she will also view her father as a resource, a wise and reliable counsel, during particularly troublesome times in her life. And, if she loses her way for a time, her father may be able to step in and bring her back to reality. Notice how Mordecai confronts Esther with the reality of life in their world:

Word of Mordecai's spectacular demonstration of grief traveled quickly through the palace grapevine. In no time at all, Esther's maids and eunuchs told her all that was happening. She was greatly distressed by the news and immediately sent Mordecai a new set of clothes to wear.

You can almost hear what Esther is thinking: *Get out of the sackcloth and ashes! I can't believe this! Do you realize that everyone in the palace is talking about the old Jew at the king's gate who is dressed in ashes and rags and is wailing bitterly? How can you tell me not to let even my husband know who I am and then turn around and do this? This makes no sense!*

Esther essentially tells him to clam up, get back in his Brooks Brothers suit, and look the part. But Mordecai flatly refuses to honor her request. Baffled by his response, Esther sends Hathach, her most trusted eunuch, to speak with Mordecai and find out why he is so upset.

"So Hathach went out to Mordecai in the open square of the city in front of the king's gate. Mordecai told him everything that had happened to him, including the exact amount of money Haman had promised to pay into the royal treasury for the destruction of the Jews. He also gave him a copy of the text of the edict for their annihilation." But Mordecai did not stop there. He also asked Hathach to explain the whole situation to Esther and "told him to urge her to go into the king's presence to beg for mercy and plead with him for her people."[3]

What a turn of events! It was apparently too dangerous for Esther to speak directly with Mordecai. After all, everyone knew he was Jewish. So Esther sent Hathach to find out what was wrong.

I find it interesting that although Mordecai had cautioned Esther about revealing her spiritual heritage, he was not afraid to boldly plead before God and man for the salvation of his people. He was grieving the upcoming loss of his people—babies, children, parents, and grandparents. He was not about to put on a happy face and pretend that nothing was happening. When Hathach approached him, Mordecai shared every detail without hesitation. He provided hard evidence for his complaint. He also made it clear that Esther needed to take a stand for her people. The interaction between Mordecai and Esther that follows demonstrates the important role a father can play in the life of his adult daughter.

By this time, Esther had been queen for several years. She was well aware of royal protocol. She probably had become aware of some of the reasons Mordecai had taught her to keep her identity a secret, for his actions obviously upset her. Her first response was to try to get Mordecai to quiet down. She frantically sought an easy way to get things back to normal.

But Mordecai greeted her actions with a full presentation of the facts. He did not live with the illusion that he could keep his daughter safe in an evil world, and he did not allow her to live with that false illusion of safety either. He knew that her best chance for survival was to be strong and to face the reality of life as it was. He knew that what had happened to Vashti could happen to her as well. I think he also knew that despite her status as queen, she had not outgrown her need for his support and guidance, particularly during a crisis. That is why he clearly explained the whole situation to Hathach and why he stated exactly what action he wanted Esther to take.

Fathers today would be wise to follow Mordecai's lead in helping their daughters face the difficult realities of life. Although we like to think of our country as a safe place, daughters today face life-and-death issues, just as Esther did. Our society, for example, doesn't uphold biblical values and standards of sexual conduct. According to contemporary societal standards, virginity and monogamous marriage are obsolete. By today's standards of intimacy, sexual intercourse carries the same significance as holding hands and kissing did in the 1950s. The fantasy is that this is the normal way to live, but the reality is twofold: God's standards for sexual conduct have not changed, and it takes only one sexual experience to contract the HIV virus. The consequence of following the fantasy today does indeed lead to spiritual and physical death. It takes an emotionally and spiritually strong young woman to maintain the boundaries necessary to look past the fantasy and deal with real life in a sexually addicted society.

Like Mordecai, fathers today need to confront personally the dangerous reality of life. They need to feel the pain, the loss, and the tragedy of those realities deep in their hearts. They need to live out the convictions of their hearts in daily life so that their daughters will know that they speak the truth and that living in the light of God's truth is important. Finally, they need to make sure that their daughters aren't taken in by the fantasy. They can accomplish this by giving their daughters a full explanation of the facts—addressing the dangers and specifically stating what their daughters need to do to remain safe.

This teaching is by no means limited to areas of sexual behavior. For instance, a father needs to help his daughter face reality in the workplace. It is no small thing to succeed in the business world today. Many young women enter the workplace thinking that if they do their work well, they will succeed. This, too, is a fantasy. The reality is that, in the world of gainful employment, a woman is likely to face sexual harassment, dishonesty, emotionally abusive supervisors, and more. To be successful, she must not only work hard and do her job well, she must also be astute in learning the unwritten rules of her workplace, how to play politics, how to promote and protect herself, and more. A father can do much to help his daughter learn these difficult, and often painful, lessons.

Dave's daughter, Jennifer, needed his help to sort through some of these issues when she started her first job. Jennifer was still in high school but worked part time in a fast food restaurant. Dave noticed that every time she talked about her job she talked about how unfair her supervisor was. Her supervisor favored the young men by consistently giving them the better shifts and rarely criticized them, but he frequently yelled at the young women on the job. After several weeks on the job, Dave's wife mentioned that Jennifer was suddenly having severe headaches on a daily basis. Dave decided he needed to talk with his daughter.

"Jennifer," he said, "are you afraid to walk away from this job?"

She burst into tears. "Daddy, you have always said to never give up. I don't want to disappoint you."

"I won't consider you a quitter if you leave this job," he explained. "It seems that your supervisor is abusive, and you should not have to put up with that. Let's see what options you have."

Together they determined that she could leave the job, confront the supervisor, or document the supervisor's behavior and pass it on to the manager and the corporate headquarters. Jennifer wanted the job and the supervisor was too dysfunctional to confront directly, so they chose the latter option. Jennifer carefully documented the supervisor's past as well as present behavior and presented it to the manager. The manager immediately changed her to a different supervisor and, since there had been previous complaints about the first supervisor, put him on probation. Within a month, the first supervisor was fired and Jennifer was given his job.

Jennifer learned many valuable lessons through this experience. She would not have learned those lessons without her father's involvement. He helped her face the reality of a difficult situation and taught her important survival skills.

There is also a place for a father to expose the fantasy his daughter may have about marriage. One widowed father who had terminal cancer found that he had to confront his daughter with reality as it related to her life and marriage. The daughter, Mary, was in her mid twenties and had been living with a young man for several years. Since her boyfriend, Bill, was a yet-to-be-discovered musician, she had been supporting him for most of their relationship. Bill had asked her to marry him, but she had declined. However, her father was concerned that she might eventually marry him and set herself up for a difficult and painful future. So he sat down and had a long talk with her about issues that were close to her heart.

"I know these past few years have been hard for you," he said. "When your mother discovered the lump in her breast and we learned that she had advanced breast cancer, it wasn't easy on any of us. It seems like all we did for the next year and a half was to go through one treatment regimen after another. And none of them stopped the cancer. Of course, my being sick on and off during that time didn't help either." He went on to talk about how difficult it must have been for her, an only child, to know that both of her parents were in ill health. He talked about the comfort her boyfriend must have given her during that scary time.

He then explained, once again, that the tumor the surgeons had removed from his brain years earlier had recurred. "This time they cannot operate," he said gently. "There is no treatment that can make me well again. I don't know how much time I will have to be with you. I don't know how much longer I will have the ability to speak or communicate with you. So I have to tell you what's on my mind now, while I still can.

"I am concerned about your future," he continued, "particularly your future with Bill. For the past three years you have supported him. During that time he has never held a job for more than a few weeks. Do you realize that if you become Bill's wife, you will have to work all of your life? It is not realistic to ever expect his work situation to change.

"Think about what you want for your future. Think about how you want to live. We have talked about how you want to get married and have children. But do you want to have to work full time to support your husband and your children? If you marry Bill, you will have to do this. Think very carefully about what your life will be like. A few short weeks after your child is born, you will have to leave that child in someone else's care so you can go back to work. Is this the life you want to live?"

Gently, the father reminded his daughter that he most likely wouldn't be alive to help her out. He then explained that a fair amount of money had been required to pay for her mother's medical bills and that his medical bills could also be expensive. "What is left after I am gone will not last very long," he concluded. "You will have to support yourself. You are a very attractive and capable young woman. You have what it takes to succeed. You do not have to fear the future, but you must think very carefully about what you want your future to be."

Mary's father did not order his daughter to do what he thought was best for her. He offered no ultimatums. He simply exposed the fantasy and confronted his daughter with the reality of her situation. Several weeks after their talk, Mary broke off her relationship with Bill.

These are just some of the ways a father can help his daughter deal with the realities of the world. As we have seen, this is a very important part of helping to nurture and protect a daughter as she matures. However, tearing down destructive fantasies and facing reality is difficult. A father cannot expect to accomplish this successfully unless he has taken the time to be emotionally and spiritually connected to his daughter. Although a father can work to establish this connection at any point in his daughter's life, it is best if he begins that process at birth rather than at puberty or adulthood. It is not a process that takes place across a fragile thread of emotional connection; it takes place across a strong, solid emotional bridge. When a father has developed a strong emotional bridge to his daughter, he has opened the gateway through which she is able to trust his wisdom during difficult times. He is then able to expose the fantasies and ground his daughter solidly in reality.

Grounding in Reality

When I think of the emotional and spiritual connection between Esther and Mordecai, I envision the Golden Gate Bridge. Such a bridge is strong and enduring. It can bear whatever needs to take place in the relationship between them. It can handle the stresses, the give and take, as father and daughter confront the fantasies and deal with the realities of life. To deal successfully with the risky realities of their world, Mordecai and Esther needed a bridge that was *at least* as strong as the Golden Gate Bridge! A weak emotional bridge simply could not stand up under the pressure.

When Mordecai explained to Hathach why he was mourning, he also asked Esther to take a potentially dangerous stand. Naturally, she was hesitant to do that. The fact was, what Mordecai had asked her to do could cost Esther her life! Esther knew the cost, so she sent Hathach back to Mordecai with the following message:

> "All the king's officials and the people of the royal provinces
> know that for any man or woman who approaches the king
> in the inner court without being summoned the king has but
> one law: that he be put to death. The only exception to this
> is for the king to extend the gold scepter to him and spare
> his life. But thirty days have passed since I was called to go
> to the king."[4]

This must have been a confusing time for Esther. Mordecai, whom she had trusted totally to guide and protect her, seemed to have lost his senses. Instead of telling her how to be safe, he told her to risk her life by approaching the king on her own! Not only that, he had always taught her to guard her identity, but now he wanted her to expose her identity—and to expose it to the very man who had decreed the annihilation of her people!

Esther had strong feelings and opinions about these new instructions, so she basically told Mordecai to "get real." She explained not only the obvious, but shared something of her personal situation that Mordecai might not otherwise know—that she wasn't sure where she stood with the king at the moment because he hadn't asked for her recently. Mordecai received her message, then sent back his answer:

> "Do not think that because you are in the king's house you
> alone of all the Jews will escape. For if you remain silent at
> this time, relief and deliverance for the Jews will arise from
> another place, but you and your father's family will perish.

And who knows but that you have come to royal position for such a time as this?"[5]

Mordecai doesn't mince any words here, does he? He essentially says to Esther, "Stop! Do not think for one minute that you became queen just because you have a pretty face. Remember who you are. You are a Jew, a child of the living God. It is He—not you, not your husband—who controls your destiny. It may be that you have been made queen for this very occasion." Wow! Mordecai didn't speak harshly, but he certainly broke through Esther's head-in-the-sand stupor! He gave her a strong dose of reality. He was not about to let her blissfully cruise along in her fantasy of security. He continued to direct her attention toward reality.

Daughters today need to be grounded in reality as well. This isn't an easy task for fathers to accomplish. It is challenging for a father to learn how to relate to a daughter. It is no small thing to understand a daughter's world, to interact with the full scope of her thoughts, feelings, and responses. One father, who has both a son and a daughter, expresses his frustration in trying to bring reality into his daughter's life: "When I have a consequence for my son, he gets angry at me and I can handle that. I understand anger. But when I have a consequence for my daughter, she cries! I end up feeling like a big jerk. It's hard to follow through on a consequence when you feel like you are wounding your own child!"

This father is right: it isn't easy to follow through, to stick with the consequences, and help a daughter deal with reality. No matter how difficult the task may be, however, it is absolutely necessary. Unfortunately, fathers who don't know how to connect with their daughters and direct them toward reality often indulge their daughters. A father who doesn't know how to give of himself, for example, will often give money to his daughter. When this happens, the father is in danger of creating a princess who has few responsibilities and doesn't know how to face the real world. Instead of helping his daughter learn how to handle life as it is, he allows her to live in an unreal world.

It is especially easy for a father to indulge his daughter in an affluent society. I see many examples of this in Southern California where I live. In some cases, it is as if the father's Nordstrom card takes the place of his involvement in his daughter's life. The daughter, armed with her father's money, is able to go out and buy a ninety-five-dollar article of clothing or a pair of shoes without a second thought. Or her father promises to buy her any brand new car she wants—complete with every option and accessory—for her sixteenth birthday.

There's no reality in this kind of "giving." The father is allowing his daughter to live an illusion. This type of treatment is a devastating wound to a young woman who eventually will have to survive in the real world. When she leaves home and begins life on her own, when her father loses his job, or when she marries a man who makes only $15,000 a year, the daughter who has been treated like a princess is in for a real shock.

It is so important for a father to teach his daughter the skills she will need to safely make her way in the world. He needs to make sure she realizes that a dollar only buys so much, that she will have to budget her spending in order to pay her bills. Before she goes out into the world, a daughter needs to know that if she spends too much money, she will get into trouble. She needs to know that if she doesn't do her work in the way her employer requires, she will lose her job. She needs to know that if she doesn't feel like fixing dinner she can't just go out and put it on a credit card. She needs to know that she must deal with life as it is, not as she would like it to be. She needs to know that she cannot escape the consequences of her actions.

The father's role in helping his daughter deal with reality is not limited to helping her deal with everyday life in this world. The father plays an important role in directing his daughter toward spiritual reality as well. Mordecai brings the spiritual reality into clear focus for Esther when he tells her that relief for the Jews will come and that she may well be the woman God has ordained to bring about that relief.

Thorough grounding in spiritual reality is necessary for survival during dangerous times. It isn't easy to come face-to-face with spiritual reality. Spiritual reality can be comforting, challenging, empowering, and frightening—and it can be all of those things at the same time. Unless we have someone who brings that reality before us and holds us accountable for dealing with it, it is all too tempting to ignore it. Mordecai, because of his relationship with Esther and his own spiritual commitment, is able to bring that reality before Esther. Notice how he does it:

- First, he reminds Esther of who God is—that God is undeniably in control and that He deeply loves His people.
- Second, he assures Esther that God will deliver His people from the evil that oppresses them.
- Third, he does not deny that some of God's people may perish before deliverance comes.
- Fourth, he clearly states the choice that is before her.

Mordecai does this in a gentle, yet powerful, way. He doesn't blame Esther for being scared. He acknowledges that these are scary times and that there is risk on all sides. Although he encourages her to take a risky, courageous step, he doesn't tell her what she must do. Instead, by pointing out the spiritual reality of what God may have in mind, he clarifies the choice that Esther must make. Furthermore, he makes it clear that the decision she makes is between her and God; she alone carries the responsibility for her decision.

This interaction speaks loudly of the strength of their relationship. The reality that Mordecai has modeled and taught has become a part of Esther's life. She is in a position where she can face the difficult realities of life and deal with them as an adult woman before God. This level of communication could not have taken place without a solid connection between father and daughter. The emotional relationship had to exist first so that father and daughter could handle the open, straightforward communication that was necessary to deal effectively with the temporal and spiritual realities of their lives.

Open Communication

It is sad, but many well-meaning fathers are unable to have the positive impact they would like to have on their daughter's lives because they lack a strong emotional and spiritual connection with their daughters. Bob, for example, was concerned about his fifteen-year-old daughter, Nancy. She had recently lost interest in her church youth group and become involved with a group of angry teenagers at school. Her dress, hairstyle, and demeanor was changing to conform to that of her new friends.

Bob had been attending a men's Bible study that focused on how fathers could improve relationships with their children, so he decided to take Nancy out for breakfast and share his concerns. As they ate, he shared his feelings about the changes he observed in her life. He talked about how he wanted to help her draw closer to the Lord. He encouraged her to become active in the church youth group again.

Bob is to be respected for taking that step, for it was more intimate than the interaction he had experienced with his father. It wasn't enough, however. The emotional and spiritual connection between father and daughter was insufficient to support honest, two-way communication on these important issues. Nancy became angry and accused her father of not trusting her. Later that night, when she was with her friends, she took an overdose of pills and nearly died.

Bob felt terrible. He had made a sincere effort to help his daughter deal with a dangerous situation, but things had not turned out as he had hoped. In fact, it seemed as if his efforts to help his daughter had caused even greater harm. Bob didn't know what went wrong. The tragedy is, Bob's relationship with Nancy was not strong enough to handle the level of communication necessary to deal with the reality they faced.

Notice the contrast between Esther and Mordecai's interaction and that of Bob and Nancy. One daughter takes her father's advice seriously while the other daughter rebels against her father's advice. Both fathers cared enough for their daughters to address difficult issues. Yet only one father had a solid enough bond with his daughter that she could take his counsel to heart. Mordecai communicated across an enduring Golden Gate Bridge, while Bob communicated across a shaky, splintering thread that stretched over a deep chasm through which a raging river boiled.

Few fathers and daughters have the strong bridge of emotional connection that is necessary to communicate on the level that Esther and Mordecai communicated. Most daughters, whether they are adults or young girls, feel a bit uneasy or fearful of straightforwardly revealing their thoughts and feelings to their fathers. Often this hesitancy comes from being shamed or in some other way wounded when feelings—particularly those of anger, hurt, or fear—were shared in the past.

When a father is not connected to his own feelings, his daughter quickly learns that it isn't safe to share her feelings with him. Unfortunately, when it is difficult or unsafe to share feelings of anger, hurt, or fear, it is also difficult to honestly share feelings of love, care, and respect. Under these conditions, the father and daughter may be able to express care and love for one another on a superficial level only. Their efforts may create the illusion of a deep, familial relationship, but the relationship has a plastic quality to it. When things get intense and hot, the relationship may melt under the pressure. Under cold, difficult conditions the relationship may become brittle and break. But when the relationship is strong enough to embrace the more difficult and painful feelings, then a deeper level of love and communication can exist.

Whenever I read the story of Esther and Mordecai, I am amazed by the depth of their communication. There is an honesty evident in their relationship that I respect and admire—an honesty I hope to emulate. It certainly isn't easy to maintain honest and respectful communication under the pressure of imminent death, but Mordecai and Esther were direct and honest in their communication with each other. Mordecai explained what he wanted Esther to do to bring relief to their desperate situation. Esther responded by expressing her fears and concerns, by saying that she did not want to die. Mordecai, in turn, responded honestly to Esther. He felt the turmoil and fear she faced, so he did not make light of her feelings. He did, however, remind her of the seriousness of their predicament and expose the false sense of security in which she was taking comfort: "Do not think that because you are in the king's house you alone of all the Jews will escape. For if you remain silent . . . "

Fascinating things happen when this kind of communication takes place. When both father and daughter choose to be vulnerable and honest in working through their feelings, the emotional and spiritual bridge between them becomes stronger. As they honestly deal with the difficult issues together, the daughter becomes better able to feel God's presence and guidance in her life. She becomes empowered to take the risks of living in the world as it is.

Remember Bob and his daughter Nancy? When Nancy was hospitalized following the pill overdose, the whole family began therapy. Bob began a recovery program from alcoholism, Nancy entered a treatment program for drug dependency, and Bob's wife began attending a twelve-step group for codependents. It took several years of hard work, but now father and daughter relate to each other on an entirely different level than was possible in the past. As Bob gained sobriety and started facing his own issues, he became more responsive to the needs of his daughter's heart. For perhaps the first time, Nancy actually felt her father's love for her. When she became confident of her father's love, she became able to listen to the wisdom he shared from deep within his heart. In time, her relationship with God the Father was back on track and she was able to make changes in her relationships with her friends.

As Esther expressed her feelings and opinions to Mordecai, she discovered some important truths about herself as well. Through Mordecai's nurturing guidance, she was able to see the truth of his difficult message. She gained the courage, as a daughter of the living God, to take a very risky stand. She became empowered to take the risks of living out her full potential in the real world.

Questions

1. In what ways has your father afforded you protection and wisdom?

2. In what ways has your father revealed his emotion or spiritual integrity to you? How did that impact you?

3. Describe a time when your father has helped you deal with reality. How receptive are you to his instruction?

4. In what ways are you and your father able to share deep and perhaps difficult feelings with one another?

5. Take a few moments to thank God for His fatherly protection and wisdom.

CHAPTER 6

Developing
Feminine Strength

*A father plays a crucial
role in nurturing his
daughter's feminine strength.*

---

*At a time when the people of Israel were greatly
oppressed by King Jabin of Hazor and Sisera, the cruel
commander of Jabin's army, there lived a prophetess
named Deborah. A married woman, Deborah lived in the
hill country, but she was more than a country wife—she
was a judge of Israel! She sat under the Palm of Deborah,
and all of Israel came to seek her judgment.*

*One day Deborah received a message from the Lord to
deliver to a man named Barak. Hers was no ordinary
message; it was a call from God for Barak to lead a rebel-
lion against Sisera and his army! Barak was understandably hesitant to take on such a task. After all, Sisera had
an army that included 900 iron chariots, and his reputation for cruelty was widely known by the Israelites who
had suffered under him for twenty years. On the other
hand, Barak didn't feel confident in disobeying the Word of*

the Lord either, so he said to Deborah, "If you go with me, I will go; but if you don't go with me, I won't go."

"Very well," she replied, "I will go with you. But because of the way you are going about this, the honor will not be yours, for the Lord will hand Sisera over to a woman." So Barak raised his army, and together he and Deborah led them into battle.

Barak's army routed Sisera's troops, but Sisera himself escaped on foot. Sisera ran to the tent of Jael, a Kenite woman, to seek refuge because the Kenites were friendly to King Jabin of Hazor. As he expected, Jael invited him in, gave him milk to drink, and hid him under a rug in her tent. Exhausted, he soon fell into a deep sleep. Then Jael picked up a tent peg and hammer and crept close to the sleeping man. In an instant she drove the peg through Sisera's head into the ground! When Barak came by in search of Sisera, Jael led him to where the dead man lay.[1]

ॐ

The *Book of Proverbs* closes with a character sketch of a woman who is worth far more than rubies. Her husband has full confidence in her. She considers land and buys it, and out of her own earnings she plants a vineyard. She is physically strong and goes about her work vigorously. She opens her arms to the poor and extends a helping hand to the needy. Clothed with strength and dignity, she has no fear of the future and can laugh at the days to come. She speaks with wisdom and is always ready to offer a kind word of instruction. A woman like this who fears the Lord is worthy to be praised.[2]

For some reason, we don't hear much about the deep inner strength of the women in the Bible. When, for example, was the last time you heard a sermon about the strength, power, and accomplishments of female Bible characters? Or, when was the last time you participated in a Bible study on what it means for a godly woman to develop her feminine strength? For many women, the reality of their God-given feminine strength has remained unrecognized and unknown. When I speak to women's groups and ask women to imagine what feminine strength means to them, I often get blank, confused looks in response. For many of us who have been raised in the traditional Christian culture, the words *feminine* and *strength* just don't seem to go together.

Yet some of the women portrayed in the Bible exhibit undeniable feminine strength. Deborah was such a powerful and respected woman of God that Barak didn't dare go to war without her. Jael must have had tremendous inner strength (and coolness under pressure!) to deal with a man like Sisera face to face and then to kill him single-handedly. I have no doubt that the woman described in Proverbs 31 has the strength to manage a home and family wisely and compassionately, direct a ministry, or manage a Fortune 500 company. And, as we will soon discover, few have ever matched Esther's diplomacy. However vague our images of feminine strength may be, I think we can readily agree that these women have it!

My desire is that these biblical accounts, which reveal some of the depth and power of godly feminine strength, will touch the hearts of women (and their fathers) who read them. These stories may inspire a woman to renew her efforts to serve the God she loves. They may fill her with a sense of awe. They may stir up a sense of pride in her heritage as a woman of God. They may cause her own well of feminine strength to rise up within her. And I hope they will encourage fathers to take seriously their responsibility to fervently nurture the strength of their daughters.

One of the tragic consequences of the low status women

have often had in society is that women generally don't feel the reality of their own value and strength. Despite a number of laws that are intended to improve the status of women, even our culture today doesn't place as high a value on women as it should. In fact, the world is basically unsafe for women. It saddens me to say it, but contemporary Christian culture often minimizes the value of women as well. Such a viewpoint is not at all biblical. Jesus died for both male and female. In His great sacrifice of love, He demonstrated that every human being—female as well as male—is a priceless treasure in His sight. Yet it is hard for a woman to know that she is a great treasure in God's eyes— that she is strong, lovable, and capable—when she has been wounded by family dysfunction or cultural shame.

Let us take a closer look at Proverbs 31. Its portrayal of a woman who has a solid identity and an unshakable inner strength that is grounded in the Lord will help us discover what feminine strength is all about. Through this passage, we will also see some of the ways a woman's feminine strength develops.

> *A wife of noble character who can find?*
> *She is worth far more than rubies.*[3]

Amazing things happen when a woman feels deep in her heart that her worth far exceeds the value of precious jewels. A woman who truly feels her innate worth as a child of the living God has the ability to take risks, the strength to take on a challenge and bring it to fruition. If she is an entrepreneur, she can go head-to-head with a Sam Walton or Tom Watson, Sr. If she is a homemaker, she delights in providing a loving and secure environment for her family. She is willing at times to sacrifice her needs for those of her family, but also finds ways to care for herself so that she continues to grow spiritually and emotionally. If she is an artist, she has a confidence in her work that empowers her to take risks to expand her creativity and to broaden her market. If she is a politician, she takes the risk of acting on her feelings and beliefs through her involvement on a local school board, state advisory committee, or other governmental position.

The ultimate foundation for this feeling of feminine value and strength comes from God. That foundation, however, is built in large part through the involvement of a father who is emotionally and spiritually connected to his daughter. Tragically, as we have seen, few fathers realize the impact they have on their daughters. Few fathers realize that a daughter takes to heart the attitudes the men in her family have toward women.

If her father, grandfathers, uncles, and others view women as weak and incapable, that is the image of women a little girl will carry in her heart. If the men who are close to the little girl believe that women are to submit to men above all else, that concept becomes the standard by which she relates to all men—even to abusive men. If, on the other hand, they demonstrate caring and compassion for others, she will learn to feel and have compassion. If her father is willing to take a stand, she will feel a sense of pride in her father's strength and realize that she can do the same. If her father allows himself to develop his creativity and learn from his mistakes, he sets the stage for her to enjoy the challenges of a lifetime of learning and creativity.

In her book, *In God's Image*, Craig Ballard Millet writes about the types of women found in Scripture. One of those women she calls "the father's daughter."[4] This woman is intelligent and has great inner strength. Millet describes her as a planner, achiever, and survivor who is not only capable, but adaptable. The father's daughter will make herself successful in whatever she chooses to do. Rather than being a victim or enemy of her father, she is well equipped to thrive in a competitive, male-dominated world. So the father who is emotionally and spiritually connected with his daughter and is involved in her life gives her a tremendous gift of value and strength.

A father who wants his daughter to have a value that is greater than her physical appearance (greater than the expense of her make-up and clothes), greater than her material accumulation (finer than the house she lives in or the car she drives), greater than her social status (more significant than her or her husband's job title), needs to invest his time, heart, and soul into her life. It is this investment and the resulting bond with her earthly father that gives a daughter the first taste of her worth and value before God.

> *Her husband has full confidence in her*
> *and lacks nothing of value.*
> *She brings him good, not harm,*
> *all the days of her life.*[5]

What a comment on marriage! The husband of this woman trusts her completely and receives personal benefit as a result of that trust. This statement implies that a deep level of trust yields great rewards. This is true in so many ways. A woman who has the freedom to discover and explore her gifts, abilities, and interests brings a gift of great worth to her relationship with her husband. He has the benefit of incredible support as he takes the risks necessary to ensure his continued growth and maturity. He has a true partner in life.

Although these verses present a beautiful image of trust, intimacy, and goodness in marriage, the marital relationship is far from simple. The kind of marriage described here doesn't happen automatically. In fact, a wife cannot "do good" toward her husband if she has experienced physical or sexual abuse from her father, if she grew up in an alcoholic home, or if she grew up in an emotionally abusive home where she received regular injections of shame and control. Before a woman can "do good" toward her husband and do so abundantly, she needs to recover from her own wounds, particularly those she suffered through relationship with her father.

Recovery is necessary because a woman cannot perceive her husband to be a safe person until she faces the hurts she received from her father and begins the process of healing the wounded child within her. When a woman feels emotional pain, she perceives her husband to be like all the men who have wounded her in the past. Emotionally she cannot feel the difference between her husband and the men who have wounded her. Her husband then receives all the anger and shame of those past experiences. When this happens, there is no way a woman can bring good to her husband.

Facing the wounds of the past is particularly difficult when the memory of those wounds has been blocked out of conscious awareness. One woman I counseled, for example, became fearful and tense whenever her husband reached toward her in bed. She was frustrated because she didn't know why she responded in that way. As we explored her childhood experiences, she became connected with memories of being sexually abused by both her father and her grandfather. No wonder she cringed at her husband's touch! To the little girl within her, touch from a man —any man—was scary. Until she dealt with what had happened, she was unable to distinguish between the touch of her father, her grandfather, and her husband. A woman who works a strong recovery program becomes able to respond with good toward her husband for a lifetime.

This passage carries not only a message for women, but one for husbands. That message is about the heart of the husband trusting his wife. In Hebrew, the word heart is *leb*, which means "inner man" or "being." So this passage indicates that this woman's husband trusts her without reservation. He trusts her from the depths of his being.

For some men, trusting a wife to be and do what she needs to do in life is a scary prospect. This is particularly true when a woman starts to face her woundedness and begins the process of emotional and spiritual healing. Her husband may become fearful and suspicious at this time. He may have difficulty dealing with strong women and feel more comfortable when he can control or dominate his wife rather than support, trust, and encourage her. This is a great loss for the woman as well as for her husband and family. An emotionally healthy woman who has a solid identity in Jesus Christ overflows with an inner strength that brings great good to her husband and family.

> *She selects wool and flax and works with eager hands.*
> *She is like the merchant ships, bringing her food from afar.*
> *She gets up while it is still dark;*
> *she provides food for her family and portions for her servant girls.*[6]

The woman described here must have had an incredible relationship with her heavenly Father, her earthly father, her grandfather, and her uncles! Do you sense how self-assured and physically confident she is? This woman knows who she is. She is connected with the physical world. She enjoys producing something through the work of her hands and does it with passion. The Hebrew word for eager is *chepets*, which means "to take delight" or "find pleasure." So this woman finds pleasure in creating garments of flax and wool.

The passion of her creativity overflows to other areas of life as well. She is competent to conduct the business necessary to manage her household, and she does so with energy and purpose. She isn't satisfied with McDonald's day after day. She wants to sample the variety of life and enjoy it. She is willing to risk in order to discover more of the delights God's world can bring.

Unlike this woman, many women have never experienced the joy and satisfaction of creating something tangible or accomplishing a physical feat. They don't know what it means to delight in their work. This is an area in which a daughter benefits greatly from her father's active involvement, because most fathers are very much involved in the physical world and gain confidence and satisfaction from their accomplishments. They may build fences or furniture, play basketball, paint the house, repair the car, scuba dive, plant a tree, or ride a bike, yet they often exclude their daughters from such physical activities because they don't consider these to be feminine activities or falsely assume that their daughters will not enjoy them. The truth is, daughters enjoy most activities in which their fathers are involved!

A daughter who has the opportunity to share in her father's interests and experiences gains much. When she, side by side with her father, discovers how to use her mind and hands to build, repair, or create something, her self-confidence grows. When she is invited to participate in her father's physical world through sporting activities, she learns important survival skills and gains confidence in her physical ability.

Mary's father, for example, enjoyed the outdoors. Whenever possible, he would don a backpack and hike into the mountains to get away from it all. When Mary was five years old, her father started taking her on short day hikes. They would explore the woods together or follow a stream as far as they could. Along the way they would stop to skip rocks across the water, to look for tadpoles and minnows, or to pick a few flowers. As Mary grew older, her father took her on longer, more strenuous hikes. He taught her how to walk so that she wouldn't tire as easily. He taught her how to safely cross a rushing stream. He taught her about the plants and animals that inhabited the areas they explored.

One weekend, when Mary was ten years old, her father took her on an overnight hike into the mountains. The chance to hike for a day and camp out under the stars and hike back to the car the next day was a tremendous experience for Mary. On Monday, when she told her friends what she had done, they could hardly believe it. When she brought pictures of their trip to school a few days later, the boys as well as the girls in her class treated her with a deeper respect. Mary knew how to hike and camp out in the mountains! The physical confidence Mary gained that weekend made a life-long impact on her.

Nancy's father, on the other hand, didn't spend much time in the mountains. His weekends were filled with construction projects at home. Ever since she can remember, Nancy was his constant companion and assistant. She would hand him the tools he asked for. She would carry wood for him. She would help him hold things in place when he needed an extra hand. She learned at an early age how to hold a hammer and measure carefully. By the time she reached adolescence, she was able to use her dad's power tools and could build simple wood projects on her own.

As she and her father worked together, Nancy learned many important lessons. One such lesson was that a mistake is only a mistake, and when you make a mistake you pick up and try again. When she cut a piece of wood the wrong way, her father would say, "It's only wood. We can begin again with another piece. I'm sure we will be able to use that piece on another project."

You don't have to look far in Nancy's life to see the impact her father had when he brought her into his world. Nancy isn't afraid to tackle any remodeling project at home. In fact, her husband came home one day to find a hole in the wall because Nancy had decided that spot was a good place for a door! She is also an excellent negotiator at work; it seems she can find a way to negotiate even the stickiest disagreements. She has strong boundaries in all of her relationships, yet is emotionally and spiritually involved with her husband and children. She is a powerful and strong woman, yet is vulnerable and tender. A woman who is able to maintain both strength and tenderness has a deep inner confidence—a confidence that in Nancy's life was nurtured during the many hours she spent woodworking with her father.

The kind of physical confidence that Mary and Nancy have is a precious gift that any father can give to his daughter. Physical confidence enables a woman to take on a task or to set a personal goal and delight in seeing it through to completion. It enables her to stand strong against forces that would harm her. Building this kind of confidence requires a father who is willing to do more than give his daughter a credit card to use at the mall. It requires a father who is willing to open the door and involve his daughter in his world.

> *She considers a field and buys it;*
> *out of her earnings she plants a vineyard.*[7]

Look at the skills this woman has! She knows how to operate a business, how to buy and sell, how to stay within a budget, how to negotiate, and how to plan for the future. This is a woman of strength! She knows her mind and knows how to take action. I don't think anyone would have gotten by with paying her less than what a man would earn for the same work. She may even have given the late Sam Walton a run for his money!

This astute business woman not only has the confidence and know how to run a business, she has vision. Notice that she didn't buy a vineyard; she bought a field and planted a vineyard. She saw a field that had potential and made that potential happen. Notice also that she didn't take out a loan for this venture; she used her earnings (perhaps from another business) to make it happen. As a young girl, she must have had someone to look up to and learn from. I can almost picture her, a child standing in the background, listening to every word and watching every movement and facial expression as her father conducts his business.

Karen, my wife, received similar training from her father. She grew up on a farm in central Minnesota and watched her father negotiate deals for farm equipment, cars, and supplies. She learned well how to hold out for the best deal possible. Her skills have served us well through the years. When I was in graduate school, for example, we needed to buy a new car. Our '78 Buick had 127,000 miles on it and, although it still had a good engine, nuisance repairs were becoming a burden. A car dealer would give us $1,000 in trade, but we needed $2,000 as a down payment on a replacement car. We had no choice but to sell the Buick ourselves.

We advertised the car in the paper and the calls soon started. Every caller asked for "the man of the house," but Karen was handling this deal because her negotiating skills are far better than mine. She would not budge from the $2,000 we were asking, so caller after caller said they were not interested. Finally, a man who owned three businesses and was in the process of buying a fourth came to look at the car. His wife really liked the car, so he offered Karen $1,500.

"No," Karen said. "We have to have $2,000."

The man countered with an offer for $1,800.

I started to get excited. *Okay, we've got a deal,* I thought.

"No," Karen said. "We need $2,000."

"You know," the man answered, "it is customary for you to come down when I move up!"

"No. We need $2,000," was all that Karen would say.

As the man left, I turned to Karen and said, "I would have taken the $1,800."

Karen firmly reminded me that we did need $2,000 if we were going to purchase another car. At that point I was beginning to think that we would have the Buick for a very, very long time. But I knew it was wise for me to let Karen handle the sale in the way she believed was best.

Two hours later, the man called and said he would buy the car for $2,000. When he paid Karen with twenty $100 bills, he complimented her on her salesmanship. Karen knew what she wanted, had strength of purpose, maintained firm boundaries, and did not waver from her goal. She gained this gift of strength from her father.

She girds herself with strength,
and makes her arms strong. [8]

Physical strength is an important aspect of feminine strength, and this woman is certainly strong. It seems that she takes special effort to ensure that she has the strength to carry her through whatever she may face in life. It is no secret that being a wife, mother, and entrepreneur requires physical strength as well as emotional well-being and spiritual wholeness. Yet it is easy for us to forget that we are emotional, spiritual, and physical beings and to neglect one or more of these aspects of life.

Many women minimize the importance of their physical strength. To some women (and their fathers), the terms *physical strength* and *feminine* don't seem to belong together, so they basically ignore the development of physical strength. Some fathers are threatened by strong women and therefore have trouble encouraging the development of their daughters' strength. Other fathers don't take care of themselves physically and therefore set poor examples for their daughters. Yet physical strength is essential if women today are to handle the stresses of school, work, marriage, or parenting. Furthermore, recent medical research indicates that regular aerobic activity and strength training can effectively prevent certain degenerative diseases such as osteoporosis.

I am thankful that I grew up on a farm where mothers, grandmothers, aunts, and sisters were physically able to do nearly any tasks that men did. Whether it was milking cows, driving tractors, handling bales or feed bags, women were just as capable as men. In fact, it often took the work of both men and women to get the crop in on time or to get the chores done in spite of a howling blizzard. These experiences early in my life gave me a respect for the physical strength of women. I, in turn, desire to communicate that respect and appreciation of feminine strength to my daughters.

A daughter benefits greatly if her father approves and affirms the development of her physical strength. Consider ways in which a father can do this:

- When he cares for himself physically, he sends a message to his daughter that physical strength is important.
- When he participates in physical activities with his daughter, such as playing ball, bike riding, running, swimming, and the like, he nurtures her confidence in her physical ability.
- When he affirms his daughter's physical strength, he fosters her acceptance of her body *as it is*, which is crucial in a culture that essentially worships physical perfection.

- When his encouragement prompts her to take on new physical challenges or push herself beyond where she has gone before, she learns that she is physically capable of withstanding the stresses and pressures of life.

Fortunate is the woman who has a father who nurtures her physical strength and confidence. This aspect of her feminine strength will serve her well as she learns to set boundaries and assert herself in the world.

> She sees that her trading is profitable,
>   and her lamp does not go out at night.
> She opens her arms to the poor
>   and extends her hands to the needy.
> When it snows, she has no fear for her household;
>   for all of them are clothed in scarlet.
> She makes coverings for her bed;
>   she is clothed in fine linen and purple.
> Her husband is respected at the city gate,
>   where he takes his seat among the elders of the land.[9]

It is hard to imagine a more successful woman than the one described here! She has it all. She not only is successful in her work, she feels good about her accomplishments. She makes sure that her family and children have what they need, but the scope of her love is not limited to her immediate family. She is also compassionate and generous to those who are poor. She has a husband who is an honorable and respected community leader. Since both husband and wife appear to be secure and successful in their individual accomplishments, they most likely are supportive of one another rather than threatened by one another.

Unfortunately, many women find it difficult to enjoy the blessings of the success God brings into their lives. Rather than enjoying and sharing the benefits of success, they may become fearful of losing what they have gained or feel that no amount of success will ever be enough. Other women learn at an early age that some men are threatened by a woman's success, so they minimize their accomplishments or hold back so that their full potential is never realized. This, sadly, is true in some marriages where the wife is expected to support and encourage her husband's success, but the husband will not encourage his wife because he feels threatened by her success.

Yet the woman described in Proverbs 31 has a deep sense of satisfaction in what she has accomplished. The New American Standard Version rendering of the passage above begins, "She senses that her gain is good." A strong woman who is emotionally secure is able to feel a healthy sense of pride and pleasure in what she has accomplished. A spiritually secure woman is able to feel blessed by the ways in which God has prospered her.

It's important to note that this woman's feeling of confident satisfaction is not self-serving. A strong, well-grounded, successful woman can see beyond her personal world and does not distance herself from the needs of others. She does not use her success to insulate her from the harsh realities of life. Like this woman, she feels deep in her heart the pain and needs of those who suffer, and in love and compassion reaches out to them. Feminine strength truly is good and beautiful.

> She is clothed with strength and dignity;
>   she can laugh at the days to come.
> She speaks with wisdom,
>   and faithful instruction is on her tongue. [10]

What a picture of feminine strength! Who wouldn't want to be like this woman? What a tribute for the Scriptures to say that she is "clothed with strength and dignity." This woman, who lived thousands of years ago, did not mature into a woman of strength and dignity through psychotherapy! These qualities must have developed through her spirituality and her extended family relationships.

Perhaps her father took great delight and pride in her strength. Perhaps he was a deeply feeling man who affirmed what she felt in her heart. Perhaps she was mentored by a similarly strong mother, grandmother, or aunt. Whatever took place in her development, it produced a godly woman of strength who inspires and encourages women even today. The strength and dignity of this woman was so much a part of her that it radiated through her appearance. Such a woman speaks with great wisdom and has much to give to her world.

I would like to know more about this woman's father. I'm sure that his example and teaching would be a great help to me and other fathers. Although we know nothing about the father of the Proverbs 31 woman, we do know something about Esther's father, Mordecai. What we know of Mordecai and how he nurtured Esther's feminine strength shows us what a father can do to build up his daughter's feminine strength.

Questions

1. How would you describe your feminine strength? In what ways would you like to develop your feminine strength?

2. How has your father's view of women affected the woman you are today?

3. What strengths or abilities, weaknesses or resentments, do you attribute to your father's involvement in your life?

4. What aspects of the Proverbs 31 woman's strength inspire you to take risks in your own life?

5. Take a few moments to thank God for the example of the godly woman in Proverbs 31.

CHAPTER 7

The Nurturing Father

Mordecai provides an inspiring example of how a father nurtures his daughter to maturity.

Queen Esther was very upset when her father Mordecai began wailing in grief at the city gate. She was even more upset when she learned the cause for his distress and the dangerous stand he wanted her to take. Didn't he know that what he was asking would result in her immediate death? Her only hope of survival was if her husband, the unpredictable King Xerxes, would grant her admission into his presence.

The young queen was deeply troubled as she considered Mordecai's grave request. She thought deeply about his words that God may very well have placed her in a royal position so that she could solicit relief and deliverance for her people. She thought about his public display of deep

grief. She thought about her identity as a Jew, one of God's chosen people. With firm resolve, she sent back this reply: "Go, gather together all the Jews who are in Susa, and fast for me. Do not eat or drink for three days, night or day. I and my maids will fast as you do. When this is done, I will go to the king, even though it is against the law. And if I perish, I perish."

When the time of fasting was over, Esther kept her word. She dressed in her royal robes and walked into the inner court of the palace—face-to-face with King Xerxes.[1]

What a powerful scene! It takes a tremendous amount of strength and conviction to walk into certain death in order to make an appeal for justice. Apparently Mordecai's actions when he learned of the coming destruction of the Jews had a powerful impact on his daughter. Mordecai did not take his spirituality lightly. He felt deeply and wasn't afraid to live out the great emotion in his heart. He modeled a level of spirituality that touched Esther's heart and enabled her to continue walking the path that lay before her.

A Model of Genuine Spirituality

Modeling is a very important part of the father-daughter relationship because what a father models either builds up or destroys his daughter. In this instance, Mordecai modeled a genuine spirituality. His actions left no doubt that he had deep feelings toward God and felt deep concern for God's people. He modeled a spirituality that showed great courage by publicly and directly expressing his grief for his people.

The honest expression of deep feelings is one gift a father can give to his daughter. When she hears her father honestly express fear or worry and take those concerns to his heavenly Father, he conveys a powerful message to her. By modeling an honest spirituality when facing the difficult realities of life, a father helps his daughter ask for help in difficult times. He helps her learn how to express her feelings to God. When she stands next to him in church and hears him sing joyful praises to God, she can feel the joy of a heart that overflows with thankfulness to God.

Christian fathers today often fail to realize the impact our actions have on our daughters. We typically consider our spirituality to be acts of worship, Bible reading, and prayer. We treat our emotions as an unrelated entity and overlook the fact that our spirituality is intertwined with every part of life. The truth is, we cannot separate spirituality from our emotions. When we praise and affirm our daughters, we convey an unspoken spiritual message that God also delights in her. When we express anger toward our daughters, we convey a spiritual message that God also may not be pleased with her. So we fathers must be keenly aware of the potential spiritual impact of our emotions on our daughters. It is important that we share the feelings of our hearts and at the same time guard the emotions that would harm our daughters. It is tragic when the emotional message we fathers send is a message we don't want to communicate.

A Test of Strength

Earlier, we saw how Mordecai broke through Esther's fantasy world and forced her to deal with reality. But he did more than bring her face to face with the real world. He also challenged her to move into new territory, to take risks that would test what she was made of. Look again at what he said to her:

"Do not think that because you are in the king's house you alone of all the Jews will escape. For if you remain silent at this time, relief and deliverance for the Jews will arise from another place, but you and your father's family will perish. And who knows but that you have come to royal position for such a time as this?"[2]

Mordecai had done much to nurture a strong daughter. He had trained her in her spiritual heritage. He had taught her how to set boundaries to protect herself. He had helped her learn to face life as it is rather than as she wanted it to be. He had been unafraid to express the deep emotion in his heart. Now it was time for Esther to discover and test the depth of her feminine strength.

This was not an easy transition for father and daughter to work through. They faced a difficult issue. As is often the case when dealing with difficult issues, they experienced an honest struggle—one on one side of the issue, one on the other. During that struggle, Mordecai had to voice strong words to Esther. Esther had to express strong emotion to Mordecai. Both of them had to hear the other's concerns. In the end, Esther, like a true leader, a queen who cares for her people, rose to the occasion. Notice her next communication to Mordecai:

"Go, gather together all the Jews who are in Susa, and fast for me. Do not eat or drink for three days, night or day. I and my maids will fast as you do. When this is done, I will go to the king, even though it is against the law. And if I perish, I perish."

So Mordecai went away and carried out all of Esther's instructions.[3]

Do you sense how strong Esther has become? At this point, she seizes her role as queen and acts on behalf of her people. She feels the reality of her position spiritually, emotionally, and physically. She knows what happened to Queen Vashti when she stood up to the king. She knows that the action she must take is like walking into a death sentence. Fear is a powerful motivator, yet Esther takes a bold step of courage. A woman of strength and valor, she fully accepts the difficult reality and is now willing to sacrifice her life for her people.

Like a true queen, Esther reveals her action plan to Mordecai and gives him his marching orders. I think Mordecai recognized at this point that Esther had been transformed into a woman of strength in her own right. I think he sensed that she had grown into her own independence and autonomy and was no longer dependent on him. Recognizing Esther as an adult woman, Mordecai stepped back from his role as father and teacher and moved into the role of father and supporter. Like a true subject, he obeyed her command without further discussion.

The Role of Support in Encouraging Feminine Strength

I admire Esther's strength in the face of a risk of incredible proportions. She has a deep conviction that taking this step of faith is the right thing to do. Despite the fact that she is in an environment where men are all-powerful and a woman's feelings, ideas, and opinions matter little, she follows her father's lead and takes a great risk. But there is something important about the way in which Esther assumes this risk: She does not do it alone. We dare not overlook the importance of adequate support if the full potential of feminine strength is to be realized.

It is beautiful that in this time of great trial and trouble Esther turns to others for support. She doesn't even consider attempting the task on her own. She knows that it requires diligent fasting on her part as well as on the part of others. So she *tells* (not *asks*) her father to enlist the help of the whole community in fasting on her behalf: "Go, gather together all the Jews who are in Susa, and fast for me." In this simple statement, the strength of the father-daughter bond shines through. Esther knows that she can trust the heart of her father. She knows that she can count on him for support, even in the face of death. She knows that he will enlist others to support her. Most important, Esther has also learned that she can turn to God in times of trouble.

The message here is clear: Strength does not mean being alone. Strength means being vulnerable to our heavenly Father and His people. Strength rises up when we share our needs, our pain, and our concerns with God and His people. One of the tragedies in the church today is that so many women try to carry their heaviest burdens alone.

Norma, for example, suffers through a secret struggle with depression. Out of the blue, with no provocation, she will start weeping uncontrollably. Although she loves her husband and children, she often feels like running away from them. She steels herself with numerous cups of coffee just to keep going through the day. Her heart is so burdened that thoughts of dying occur frequently. Confused and afraid, she can't understand how she can be a Christian and have these feelings. She is too embarrassed to talk to her pastor. She is afraid to make an appointment with a therapist. She hasn't been to her family doctor in years and now, even though she thinks she feels a lump in her breast, she's too afraid of what he might say to schedule an appointment. She doesn't know how or where to find help.

Claudia isn't too terribly different. She doesn't quite know why, but she is becoming increasingly angry at her husband. She has become irritated by his lack of emotional involvement with her and the children. She has just about had it with his lack of initiative at work because if only he would care a little more, he could be a much better provider for his family. She is becoming bitter about his lack of commitment to spiritual leadership in the home. Now her anger is beginning to frighten her. She takes it out on the children more and more. She doesn't feel she can talk to her friends about what is happening to her because lately she has even been angry at them.

Debbie is angry too—not at her family, but at God. She is successful in her career, but at thirty-eight years of age she still hasn't met a man she feels she could marry. What really irritates her is that although she has had plenty of opportunities to do otherwise, she is still a virgin—and there isn't even one, single, godly man in her church. Sometimes she feels as if she should just throw in the towel and compromise what she has always viewed as a godly way of life. Although she is respected at church and is now reaping some of the rewards of her hard work at the office, she is increasingly dissatisfied with both church and work.

Although their individual circumstances vary, all three of these women have the same problem. They are trying to make it alone, without the support of others. It is so tempting to remain silent and alone when we deal with the deep, painful issues of our hearts. It is tempting to silence the real hurts and struggles inside by compulsively overeating, relying on prescription drugs, having a few calming drinks to make it through the day, or by bingeing, purging, or starving. It is tempting to silence the rage of an abusive father by pushing the memories deeper and deeper inside. It is tempting to silence the devastation of an alcoholic spouse by working overtime to make sure that life runs smoothly anyway. But such silence is deadly, and support from others is often needed to break the silence. In Esther's case, she was tempted to remain silent and hope that she wouldn't fall victim to the coming devastation. Mordecai, however, had a strong enough relationship with Esther that he could help her see the destructiveness of her passive response.

In the same way that Esther needed the support of her father and people, Norma, Claudia, and Debbie also need the support of others. They each need someone to break through their fantasy that life will be okay if they do nothing. They each need someone who can help them realize that it is okay to ask for help. They each need someone to help them realize that the outer image cannot maintain its neat appearance if the inner reality is spiraling out of control. Norma needs to be able to share the fearful depth of her feelings with others so she can stop self-medicating herself with coffee and begin to deal with the roots of her depression. Claudia needs a safe group of women with whom to share her anger—perhaps a Codependent's Anonymous or Overcomers group that can help her stop trying to change her husband, help her direct her anger appropriately, and help her begin a recovery program. Debbie needs to become part of a supportive group of Christian women who recognize her struggle, who can grieve with her, who will be with her in her loneliness, and who will affirm her values.

It isn't easy for women today to proclaim their need for support and help. So often women put the needs and feelings of others first. After all, this is the Christian thing to do, isn't it? Yet Esther's proclamation for support ought to encourage us to make our needs known.

The fact that Esther made such a great request indicates that she had a strong connection with her earthly father and a solid faith in her heavenly Father: ". . . fast for me. Do not eat or drink for three days, night or day I and my maids will fast as you do." This was no casual, "please say a quick prayer for me" type of request. Fasting for three days is serious business. Esther and the women closest to her were going to do it, and the step was risky enough that Esther wanted the support of the entire religious community as well. At the end of the prescribed time, Esther felt enough faith in God, enough inner strength, and a strong enough resolve to take the risk. Well aware that she might fail and die, she accepted the challenge.

Feminine Strength Is Sufficient

The moment of truth came when Esther walked into King Xerxes' court and approached him face to face:

> On the third day, Esther dressed in her royal robes and went to the king's hall. When the king saw her, he was pleased with her and held out to her the gold scepter that was in his hand. So Esther approached and touched the tip of the scepter. He then asked her what she wanted, but before she could answer, he offered her up to half of his kingdom—just for the asking![4]

Can you imagine how hard Esther's heart must have been beating? One moment she doesn't know if she will live or die, and the next she is offered half of the kingdom! This is no place for weak boundaries or faltering strength, and Esther handles the situation beautifully. Now an adult woman and queen of her people, she has approached the king with a wise and calculated plan. Clearly focused on her task, she ignores his offer of wealth and power. Esther simply asks the king if he and his top man, Haman, will have lunch with her.

King Xerxes eagerly agrees, and a short time later they are enjoying the meal Esther had prepared. During the meal, the king again asks her what she wants. He tells her that no matter what it is, she can have it. He even repeats his offer to give her half of the kingdom. Even with this temptation, Esther does not waver. She graciously and cleverly asks the king and Haman to join her again for lunch the next day:

> "If the king regards me with favor and it pleases the king to grant my petition and fulfill my request, let the king and Haman come tomorrow to the banquet I will prepare for them. Then I will answer the king's question."[5]

Of course, the king accepts her second invitation. How could he refuse? Esther knows exactly what she is doing. She is honoring the king, which we know delights him. By her refusal to reveal immediately what is on her mind, she becomes a bit mysterious and intriguing to him. With his curiosity aroused, he will be eager to meet with her. Haman also is delighted and goes home feeling very proud of himself.

The next twenty-four hours are eventful. Haman's hate for Mordecai reaches its climax when, at the suggestion of his wife and friends, he builds a gallows on which to hang Mordecai. In high spirits the next morning, Haman goes to the king to ask to have Mordecai put to death. Before he speaks, however, the king asks for his advice.

During the night, King Xerxes had read the official account of how Mordecai had uncovered the plot on his life. When he realized that Mordecai had never been honored for his great deed, he determined to honor him. Haman had just entered the court when the king asked him how a person who had done a great service to the king should be honored. Assuming that he was the one to be honored, Haman made the honor as regal as possible. To his great dismay, Xerxes then asked him to personally bestow that honor on Mordecai.

Afterward, Haman rushed home in great humiliation. While he and his friends were bemoaning his certain ruin, he was whisked away to Esther's banquet. With these scenes fresh in mind, Esther dropped her bombshell:

"If I have found favor with you, O king, and if it pleases your majesty, grant me my life—this is my petition. And spare my people—this is my request. For I and my people have been sold for destruction and slaughter and annihilation. If we had merely been sold as male and female slaves, I would have kept quiet, because no such distress would justify disturbing the king."

King Xerxes asked Queen Esther, "Who is he? Where is the man who has dared to do such a thing?"

Esther said, "The adversary and enemy is this vile Haman."[6]

When Esther made this statement, the king was so enraged that he had to leave the room. Haman was terrified and clung to Esther, begging for his life. At this point we see the full power of Esther's strength. Haman knew he was doomed. With tears in his eyes, he begged for his life. Did Esther think, *Oh, poor Haman. Look how sorry he is. I don't think he will kill any more Jews. It will be okay if we let him live now.* No! Esther did not rescue Haman or try to fix things. She let the consequences fall where they needed to fall.

When it appeared that things couldn't get any worse for Haman, the king returned. He took one glance at what was happening and assumed that Haman was molesting Esther, so Haman's death sentence was sealed. After Haman's death, the king gave all of Haman's wealth to Esther. He next wrote a new decree that allowed the Jews to kill anyone who might attack them. With great celebration, all of God's people were delivered.

As I read the closing passages of Esther's story, I am struck by the magnitude of the risk she took. I am amazed by the depth of her courage as she made her appeal in the presence of these powerful and vengeful men. She was physically alone when she exposed the treachery of Haman's plot, but spiritually and emotionally she had an arsenal behind her. She carried in her heart a lifetime of experiences with her earthly father. She carried with her the support of her people. She carried in her heart the spiritual reality of her heavenly Father.

Through this story of a father and a daughter, we see how a father connects with his daughter spiritually and emotionally. We see a father who seeks out his daughter, who helps her learn about boundaries, who encourages her, who models what he teaches, and who has absolute confidence in her. We also see a daughter, who before our eyes is transformed from a child to a queen—a woman of God. We see her grow into a woman who has a strong spirituality, an unquenchable inner strength, and a bold courage—a woman who has the strength to take the ultimate risk.

Questions

1. What characteristics has your father modeled for you?

2. What are the "difficult issues" you have faced with your father?

3. How willing and able are you to accept the support and assistance of others during life's hard times?

4. How has your father helped you develop the inner strength to act with strength, courage, and independence?

5. Take a few moments to reflect on your feminine strength. In what ways has your inner strength been put to the test?

CHAPTER 8

Facing the Loss, Healing the Wounds

Wounded daughters can find healing and fulfill their God-given potential.

My tears are trapped beneath the glaze, beneath my blurring eyes,
My muscles tense, to keep restraint, for fear the rage should rise.
My quivering lips betray the fear I tried so hard to hide.
I'm numb in helpless effort, to keep it all inside.

I feel the wet of tears that fall, the red of blood that bleeds.
Though others cannot see it, my world is real to me.
Inflicting pain I find release, from torment deep within.
It doesn't seem to matter if they label it as sin.

The burn is warm, with sweet relief, I feel the twinge of pain.
It's easier to keep the hurt, than give away the blame.

I spit back out that thing which brings a sense inside of
comfort.
I don't deserve to soothe the pain. It seems so right to
hurt.

Oh angry child inside of me, you needn't bear the shame.
There is someone who understands, you know His pre-
cious name.
He sees the tears that never fall. He knows the rage in-
side.
He's felt the fear that torments you, the helplessness you
hide.

Remember child, the promise: He's not like other men.
Jesus holds you safe inside. You won't be hurt again.

Silent Rage, author anonymous[1]

Written by a bulimic, this poem symbolizes the pain many women, to a greater or lesser degree, feel inside. Efforts to numb that pain may range from anorexia to compulsive overeating, from alcoholism to compulsive service to others, from sexual addiction to codependency, from workaholism to exerting control, or from passivity to perfectionism. The causes of the pain may vary as well. They may include abandonment, shame, physical abuse, verbal abuse, emotional distance, sexual violations, rage, and the like. Yet no matter how varied the circumstances surrounding the pain may be, two things are certain. First, although the pain may have originated through a wide variety of relationships and experiences, some of it finds its source in a woman's relationship with her father. Second, as the author of the poem discovered, there is healing for the pain. That healing ultimately comes from God the Father.

Beth, for example, has a good job and a loving husband but lives on the verge of paralyzing fear. She has had these fears for as long as she can remember. Although her family was in church every time the doors opened, her parents fought continually. Beth grew afraid of her father's anger and soon learned not to ask him for anything. She remembers always feeling on edge as a child but began to relax when she married and moved out of her parents' home. That relief isn't perfect, however. All it takes is a change in her husband's voice or an unexpected demand for immediate performance from her supervisor, and Beth feels so panicked inside that she can hardly function. She feels as if she has done something terribly wrong—just as she felt when she was a little girl and faced her father's anger.

Mary's father died when she was quite young. Now, at age thirty-five, she is about eighty pounds overweight. "People at church make comments about my weight," she says. "They tell me that if I just give it over to the Lord I will be okay, but I'm not so sure. I've already tried everything. I've been to diet centers, weight-loss programs, Bible studies, and prayer groups. I can be 'good' with food for a while, but then I start feeling tense and worried. The only thing that makes me feel better is to eat. I just wish my father were still alive. I can't believe how much I miss him."

June is in her late forties but still feels unsure of herself —like a timid, little girl. Her father was always home at 5:15 but went immediately to his workbench in the garage until it was time to eat. He would eat dinner with the family, then retreat to the garage until bedtime. Meanwhile, June and her brothers had to deal with the rage of her alcoholic mother. "Dad always attempted to please Mom," she says, "and he never stood up to her when she screamed at us for just being kids. I wish he would call me to ask me how I am doing. It would mean so much if he would just recognize me as an adult and want to talk with me."

Each of these stories has a common thread: a father who was not emotionally available to his daughter. Each of these women has a hole in her soul that God designed the father to fill. As we have seen, that hole is a gaping, empty wound that longs to be filled. There are many directions a woman's search to fill that wound can take. Some women have sought fulfillment through relationships with the perfect man. Others have fallen victim to compulsive illnesses (such as bulimia) and addictions that destroy them spiritually, emotionally, and physically. Others have pursued achievements, accomplishments, and success to fill the nagging emptiness. Still others have chosen to take care of other people in hopes that someone will in turn care for them and soothe their pain.

The truth is, there is only one way to heal the wound. Healing comes through a journey into the pain of the loss of the relationship with the father. This journey involves a commitment to sobriety from whatever substance, activity, or person a woman has used to fill her emptiness. It involves learning to share with other women the deep hurt that has been longing for expression. Ultimately, it involves the willingness to take one's hurt to God the Father and allow Him to be the perfect father that no little girl has ever had. This journey, or recovery process, can bring a lifetime of growth and healing. It is a journey from which every woman can benefit.

The Risk and the Reward

There comes a time in life when a journey toward healing becomes nearly inevitable. During her twenties, a woman is preoccupied with finding her place in the world. By the time she reaches her mid thirties, she is fairly established in life and begins to take stock of where she is. The idealism and illusions she had about work, life, and marriage have generally been replaced by a sometimes-difficult-to-accept reality. By the time she reaches her forties, she begins to realize that life isn't forever and starts questioning how she is going to live the rest of her life. She may wonder if there is a better way to deal with the difficulties she faces.

While the woman in her late thirties and forties considers her state of life on the conscious level, unconscious physical and psychological processes push her to take steps toward healing as well. Her well-practiced coping strategies don't work as effectively as they once did. The pain of destructive relationships or lifestyle patterns intensifies, crying out for resolution. Her body also starts to show, through illness or disease, the physical impact of internal pain and tension. There is no escape. Psychological death eventually leads to physical breakdown. A woman must choose to reinforce her denial or to face the difficulties head on. In some cases, a woman is forced to make that choice because she faces a potentially life-threatening, stress-related physical symptom. The good news is that when a woman begins to move toward spiritual and emotional healing, she moves toward healing for physical problems as well.

The journey toward healing brings out a woman's core self. Traditionally, a woman has often been viewed (by herself and others) in terms of her roles rather than in terms of who she is as a person. A woman, for instance, may be viewed as a wife, a mother, a teacher, an athlete, a waitress, a scholar, or a corporate executive. Although there is nothing wrong with a woman functioning in these roles, they certainly do not represent the full scope of her person. A mother may also be a brilliant administrator. A corporate executive may also be a creative and passionate artist. A waitress may also be a powerful prayer warrior. Yet it has often been difficult for a woman and those around her to discover 'the other woman' behind the role she plays. As a woman does the work of recovery, however, she discovers more of the person she is inside and becomes able to more fully utilize her gifts and develop her unique potential.

When a woman begins to discover her core self, she often finds great delight in pursuing new creative, spiritual, or intellectual endeavors. I have seen women create businesses that reflect their personal interests and unique abilities. I know one woman who leads a Bible study and prepares as extensively as many pastors do for their Sunday morning sermons. I have seen women go back to school and earn degrees that enable them to fulfill a dream they had at one time given up. It's no secret that women who are in recovery generally function better in their established roles and in the fulfillment of their unique gifts.

Recovery brings relational blessings as well. When a married woman takes steps toward healing, her relationship with her husband can be better than it has ever been. Even if her husband is destructive, her ability to maintain strong boundaries that keep the relationship safe for her and for her children is greatly enhanced. When her children have an emotionally intimate relationship with a healthier, more wholly developed mother, they see a more complete picture of what it means to be feminine. Her sons will have a greater appreciation of and respect for feminine, and her daughters will be more likely to develop their full feminine potential.

Of course, change and healing are not without risk, and those risks can be terrifying. A husband, particularly, may feel threatened by his wife's steps toward recovery. As his wife begins to change and grow into who she really is, a husband may fear that he will be left behind or abandoned by her. He may become angry that she isn't the same person anymore. He may try to sabotage her efforts toward healing.

In all my years of counseling, however, I have yet to see anything but good come out of changes brought about through a solid journey into healing. In fact, I believe some recovery work is almost necessary in order for a husband and a wife to become "one flesh," which is how Scripture describes the marriage relationship.[2] We all live by the old rules we learned from the families in which we grew up. In order to leave our parents' way of doing things, we have to face what really happened in our relationship with our parents—the bad as well as the good. When we do that and let go of our family dysfunction, we can begin to see our spouse as the person he or she really is. If we do not leave our family dysfunction behind, we are limited to viewing our spouse through the distortion of our wounds and living life as victims of our pain.

A woman who pursues a journey of healing will at times face difficult risks in other areas of life. Shirley, for instance made great progress in her recovery until she had to deal with a new supervisor at work. Shirley had been with the company for years and had earned a solid reputation as a good and trustworthy worker. When she had a question or problem, she was free to speak directly with the president of the company about her concerns. Her new supervisor, however, operated through power, control, and fear. He told Shirley that she was no longer to have direct access to the president—all questions were to be discussed with him, and if she did not respect his authority he would make things very difficult for her.

As it turned out, Shirley's new supervisor made things

difficult for her anyway. He frequently blamed her for failures that were ultimately his problem, not hers. Shirley knew that these failures eventually would damage the company, but her supervisor had forbidden her to speak with anyone about it. She felt trapped—unable to do the best job for her company and unable to thwart her supervisor's negative perception of her. She was dreadfully afraid that she would lose her job.

I had worked with Shirley long enough to know that she had a rock-solid place in the company and that it would take more than this newcomer to make things go badly for her. So I worked with her to strengthen her boundaries with her supervisor. She learned to clearly express what she had done and what her supervisor had not done. She gathered the courage to politely, but firmly, state that she would not be talked to in a degrading manner and then to leave the room. The first time she set boundaries like this, her supervisor exploded like Mt. Vesuvius! Shirley simply stood her ground and documented the incident. When she had a big, fat folder of documentation, I told her to reveal what had been going on to the president of the company.

The president of the company respected Shirley. When she told him what had been happening, he was irate! He immediately went in and danced all over Shirley's supervisor. These were scary, unsettled times for Shirley. Her supervisor was furious with her and in a short time was back to his old tricks. Shirley had to be strong in maintaining the boundaries she had set. She had to face the fear of losing her job each time she stood up to her supervisor. Eventually she went to the president of the company again, armed with another folder of documentation. After this happened several times, her supervisor was fired.

Shirley was relieved when things turned out as they did, but no one can control how others will respond to growth and change, so there is always a risk that the disastrous results we fear may come about. But in spite of these risks, the journey toward healing is worth the cost. Pearl S. Buck is credited with saying, "Those who do not know how to weep with their whole heart don't know how to laugh either." Healing from the crippling wounds of the past does bring weeping with the whole heart, but it also brings a new fullness and wholeness to life—physically, emotionally, and spiritually.

Consider what happened to Annette. When she was six years old, her father left her with her alcoholic mother and took her younger sister to live with him. Annette watched her father, who was a wealthy doctor, remarry and develop a whole new life for himself and her sister. Meanwhile, Annette's life was a continuous nightmare. She weathered one crisis after another. Although she and her mother attended the same church throughout her childhood, they moved nineteen times in thirteen years because Annette's mother never had enough money to pay the bills. They lived in one place until they were evicted or until the bill collectors learned where they were, then they would move again.

Annette always felt that she was a failure, that something was wrong with her. *After all*, she would think, *if I had been good enough, Dad would have taken me to live with him, too.* At times Annette even thought she was the reason her mother couldn't pay the bills. As a result of these wounds in her relationship with her father and mother, Annette made devastating choices in her relationships with men. Her first two husbands were angry, controlling, alcoholic men. They were both abusive, and by the end of her second marriage Annette knew she needed help just to survive. That's when she began counseling and embarked on an active recovery program.

Annette's journey of healing completely changed her life.

She developed a spiritual connection with God that she had never experienced before. She not only viewed herself differently, she viewed men differently, too. Eventually she began dating a man in her church choir. Before they were married, Annette would come into my office, just beaming. "Earl," she would say, "I feel like I'm sixteen! I go out with this man and it's like I've never been on a date before. I've been married twice, but I feel like this is my first marriage!"

"That makes sense to me, Annette," I would say. "In a way this is your first marriage. It is the first time you have consciously chosen to marry a man. In your first two marriages you did nothing more than live out the pain of your relationship with your parents."

The Process of Recovery

Like Annette, many women (and men, too) spend their lives living out the pain of their wounded relationships with their parents. In an effort to maintain their own sanity, they often turn to behaviors and actions that lessen the pain they feel. These pain-numbing behaviors include codependency, toxic relationships, and a host of addictions—everything from prescription drug abuse to sexual addiction to alcoholism to compulsive work.

These behaviors provide a very shaky foundation for living. They do nothing to build up the core self of the person. They do nothing to fortify the boundaries that protect the core self from harmful attack. They do nothing to heal the painful wounds. They simply mask the pain that threatens to overwhelm the person. Eventually, codependent and addictive behaviors do one of two things: they physically destroy the person, or the pain becomes so great that no amount of codependency or addiction can keep it at bay.

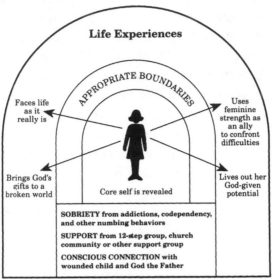

Life Experiences

APPROPRIATE BOUNDARIES

Faces life as it really is

Uses feminine strength as an ally to confront difficulties

Brings God's gifts to a broken world

Core self is revealed

Lives out her God-given potential

SOBRIETY from addictions, codependency, and other numbing behaviors

SUPPORT from 12-step group, church community or other support group

CONSCIOUS CONNECTION with wounded child and God the Father

Solid Foundation
Woman in Recovery

In order to recover and heal from this damage, a woman needs to replace the shaky foundation on which she has been living with a rock-solid foundation. A solid foundation will enable her to heal from past wounds and establish appropriate boundaries that will allow her core self—the beautiful, unique individual God created her to be—to grow and impact the world around her. A solid foundation for living consists of three parts:

- **Sobriety** from addictions, codependency, toxic relationships, and other pain-numbing behaviors.
- **Support** from a twelve-step group, church community, or other support group.
- **Conscious Connection** with the wounded inner child and God the Father.

All three elements are necessary for long-term healing and recovery to take place. If we neglect any one of these foundational areas of recovery, our healing will be hindered. We need sobriety so that we can feel the pain that is hidden in our hearts. Unless we feel our pain, we cannot identify or heal from the wounds that have hindered our growth. We need support because none of us have the personal resources and strength required to fight this battle on our own. The wisdom, encouragement, acceptance, and comfort of others can keep us on track so that we do not give up on the healing process and fall short of what God has created us to be. We need a conscious connection with our wounded inner child and our loving Father so that we can feel what takes place inside our hearts. Insight and awareness of our wounds is insufficient to bring about change and growth; we need to *feel* the impact of our wounds in the core of our being.

It is no small thing to rebuild a solid foundation for living. In fact, it is difficult enough that many of us try instead to build our lives on the shaky foundation of codependency or addiction. We all want the quick fix, the easy solution, the magical cure. We truly envy those who receive instant deliverance through God's grace and healing.

Yet the fact that there is no quick fix, that recovery is hard work, should not discourage us. Our God is vitally concerned about all that happens in the depths of our hearts. He sent His Son to die so that our hearts could be healed. He cares not only about us individually but about His whole Church—all those who call themselves Christians. I believe He wants us to support one another in all areas of life, just as the early Christians did. This support is nothing short of a life-and-death matter. A rock-bottom, honest spirituality in which all pretense is gone, all shame is gone, all blame is gone, and in which God's people honestly seek Him and support one another is what God intends. Such relationships with God and with one another bring healing. They are what bring us to life—spiritually, emotionally, and physically.

Confronting the Feelings, Choosing Healing

As I have said before, it is impossible to do the work of healing and recovery unless we first feel what is in our hearts. But the fact is, our inner feelings often cause us to feel uncomfortable and out of control. We don't like feeling that way, so we deny our feelings and block them from our conscious thought or engage in codependent and addictive behaviors that help mask the unpleasant feelings. This is something we learn to do early in our childhood. Some of us are very successful at minimizing the impact of our feelings on a conscious level, but we ultimately cannot escape from our deepest feelings. They leave their mark on us no matter what we do.

You see, the feelings to which we are exposed (through our interaction with our parents and others) and what we feel in response interact with our central nervous system and create powerful emotions, called *affect states*, that we can actually feel physically. Affect states include fear, anger, pain, and shame. They can cause an array of physical symptoms that include tightness in the stomach, clammy palms, perspiration, increased heart rate, changes in body temperature, shallow breathing, and lightheadedness—just to name a few.

Affect states can be triggered by events as seemingly benign as a slight hand movement, a song, a change in tone of voice, a facial expression, or a particular choice of words that mimics or suggests a past, painful event. The association with the past triggers the emotions of the past. Immediately the affect state takes over and produces the physiological changes described above. An individual's natural response is to engage in whatever behaviors seem to restore a sense of comfort or calm. The tragedy is that codependency or compulsive, addictive behaviors are often the quick fixes that seem to smooth out those unsettling feelings. As a result, many of us are not consciously aware of affect states until they impact us or others in a toxic way.

Allow me to use a personal example of the power of affect states on our lives. My grandfather was in his early thirties during The Great Depression years. Although he survived, he lived the rest of his life in unending fear of total economic disaster and personal failure. His fears impacted every member of my family. At times, the same fears my grandfather lived under also gain a powerful grip on me. I then feel compelled to work longer and harder and to eat more satisfying foods in order to keep the fear at bay. During those times, I need the support of others so that I can turn away from the urge to work and eat until everything is well again. I have to work very hard in order to release my fears into God's hands and to trust Him to meet my needs.

My situation is not unique. Many adults carry feelings that were induced by the families in which they grew up. One adult may experience panic attacks. Another may tend to be suspicious of people in general. Another may have trouble sleeping for fear of nighttime abuse. These are just a few of the feelings that trigger affect states.

We often think of affect states as being negative or sinful, but the truth is these feelings are not volitional. We will feel them in one way or another whether we want to or not. Although we can never free ourselves from the reality of these feelings, we can (and must) learn to recognize and confront them so that we no longer respond to them in destructive ways. That is why sobriety is essential to the healing process. We cannot recognize and confront these feelings for what they are when we expend our life's energies trying to hide them.

Impact of Family Learning on Our Feelings

Carried Feelings	Affect State	Gift
Panic, Fear, Terror	FEAR	Wisdom & Protection
Rage, Depression	ANGER	Power & Energy
Hopelessness	PAIN	Growth
Worthlessness	SHAME	Humanness

It is also helpful to realize that affect states are, by God's design, a part of our humanity. They are a gift from God and have an important function in our lives. Fear is a warning signal that cautions us to see if it is safe to proceed as planned. Anger is a source of strength that enables us to take firm action. Pain is a signal that we need healing and comfort. Shame is a reminder of our imperfect humanity. As we consider each of these affect states, it is easy to see that they force us to choose a path that leads toward further dysfunction and destruction or one that leads toward the gift of healing.

When we are in pain, for example, we have a choice to make. We can choose whatever activity enables us to ignore our pain, or we can choose to feel the depth of our pain and draw closer to God for His comfort and healing. Emotional pain can result from feelings of hopelessness, but the gift of God in the midst of pain is growth! But in order to grow, we first have to face our pain and hopelessness.

The same is true of the other affect states. We can choose to live in debilitating fear, or we can discover God's gift of wisdom and gain the ability to set protective boundaries. We can direct anger inward and become depressed, we can direct anger outward in rage, or we can face the anger and discover a new strength and energy for pursuing righteousness. We can feel shame and spiral deeper into feelings of worthlessness, or we can accept our humanity and discover the grace of making mistakes and making amends. The challenge is that in order to gain the benefit of the gift, we have to choose to face our feelings and turn away from the toxic expression of affect states.

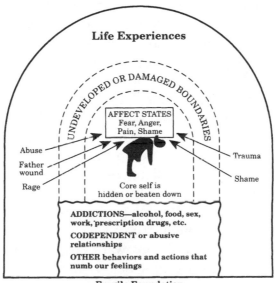

Fragile Foundation
Woman Without Recovery

Support for Recovery

As you can see, recovery is hard work. We cannot do it alone. We need the encouragement of others to maintain sobriety, and we need the support of others to face the deep feelings we harbor inside. Since we have been wounded through our relationships with others, it is naturally tempting to seek healing in isolation—apart from those who could hurt us. Healing for the deep wounds of the heart and spirit, however, comes through relationships with others.

Do you remember the Bible story about the crippled man who waited by the pool of Bethesda for thirty-eight years but never made it to the healing waters in time?[3] This man knew what he had to do to be healed. He was doing his best to be healed. Still, he could not succeed. He needed someone to wait beside him, pick him up, and carry him the last few steps into the pool. Without support from others, we, too, are like the crippled man. We may make it to a certain point in our recovery but are helpless to take the next step on our own. With the help of others, what has in the past been impossible can happen at last.

When Marla came to me for counseling, she suffered from severe depression and panic attacks. By her own admission, she had a problem with food. She had been through a number of hospital programs for her depression and had established a familiar pattern. She would get a little better, begin to feel spiritually renewed, and assume that she was all better. At that time, she would drop out of her support groups, discontinue counseling, stop taking medication, and soon begin a downward decline. Although she was highly motivated to get better, she couldn't make a long-term change.

I explained to Marla that she had an eating disorder and that the foods she usually ate simply intensified her depression and anxiety symptoms. I outlined a recovery program for her that included counseling, sobriety, and support. She wasn't convinced that this new approach would be any different from what she had tried before, but she grudgingly began to attend Overeaters Anonymous (OA) anyway.

One day at a time, Marla learned to stay free of sugar and her favorite binge foods. She began to lose weight. By actively working the twelve steps, she renewed her relationship with the Lord. Then she began to remember the times her father had abused her.

This was an extremely difficult time for Marla. The urge to use food to numb those feelings was powerful. At times she was tempted to remain silent about her painful memories. But through OA, she obtained the resources to maintain sobriety from pain-numbing, depressive foods. She also became involved in a support group for survivors, so in the middle of the night when the flashbacks of abuse would come back to her, she was upheld by women who held her, sobbed with her, and prayed for her. In time she became very aware of her heavenly Father's deep love for her. She experienced healing spiritually, emotionally, and physically in a way she never imagined possible. She was able to let go of the painful memories of her earthly father and fully embrace her heavenly Father.

Did OA play a role in her recovery? Yes! Did her survivors' group play a role? Yes! Did her pastor play a role? Yes! Did her therapist play a role? Yes! Did her family physician play a role? Yes! Did her church play a role? Yes! Could God have healed Marla without all of the above? Yes! Yet He chose to make His presence known to her through all of those people who supported her.

We cannot underestimate the role of adequate support in the healing process. It is particularly important for women who seek healing for wounds suffered in their relationships with their fathers. When a man deals with the wounds of the father-son relationship and is mentored by an older man, he establishes an emotional and spiritual connection with a father-like figure.[4] This relationship can bring about significant healing, particularly if there is little hope for the son to connect with the father. It is highly unusual, however, for a woman to have a mentoring or father-like relationship with an older man other than her father. When a woman's father is emotionally incapable of such a relationship, it is essential that she receive support from other women.

This is not to say that a woman cannot receive support from men. There can be times when male mentoring or support is very helpful in nurturing a woman's personal growth. Support may come from a professor who takes an interest in a woman and delights in the growth of her knowledge and wisdom. Mentoring may come from a male colleague who is able to guide a woman toward success in her career. Encouragement may come from a pastor who is able to communicate God's truth with deep feeling and passion. Support may also come through a compassionate family doctor.

For example, I have seen my friend, Dr. Hawkins, put his arm around a woman who is distressed and talk to her. When he does this, he doesn't give just a quick squeeze; he gives a firm hug while he talks to the person. "God is going to be with you through this thing," he may say. "You will make it through this difficult time." There is tremendous power and hope in that kind of male support, but a woman must have strong boundaries because there is risk in these relationships as well.

This is one reason I am such a strong advocate of support groups. There can be no secrets when a woman is involved in a good support group. When she is able to share everything that is happening in her life with her support group, everyone benefits. At times a man who has a supportive relationship with a woman (a physician, pastor, or therapist, for example) will violate her boundaries. When that happens, the man thinks he has control of the relationship, which allows some terribly destructive relationships to go on for a long time. But when a woman has accountability and support from other women, boundary violations and the secret behaviors that result have little chance of survival.

I have come to view support as an issue of health, an issue of the soul, and an issue of the mind. At times God instantly heals people who have suffered life-long hurts and serious illnesses. But the greatest number of people must learn to draw on God's grace and the support and encouragement of others so that they can progress toward healing one day at a time. Support is essential on a daily journey of recovery. Healing is hard work. We need someone with whom to share our deep griefs, our fears of failure, our worries about the future, our recent setbacks, our hopes and expectations, and our feelings of anger. A therapist alone cannot provide enough support for healing. A consultation with a pastor is not enough support. A visit to a physician is not sufficient. Daily, faithful support from others can work miracles in healing hurts and changing lives.

Alcoholics Anonymous is a sixty-five-year-old testimony to the fact that people who agree to honestly share with one another and to be vulnerable to God can achieve long-term sobriety. Overcomer's Outreach, a church-based support group that started only a decade ago, is a testimony to the fact that the Church today can bear the burdens of those who hurt. Bearing one another's burdens was a normal part of life in the early Christian Church. Material needs, spiritual needs, and emotional needs were met within the context of the Christian community. In more recent times, however, the Church has focused primarily on meeting spiritual needs and secondarily on meeting material needs. The concept of meeting emotional needs has in many respects been ignored. As a result, God's people have suffered. The church today would do well to reestablish its role in bearing all of one another's burdens—the emotional as well as the spiritual and material.

Healing Connections

With a background of sobriety and support, the feelings of the wounded girl inside will begin to surface. These feelings may rise up spontaneously without conscious effort. They may present themselves within the safety of a counseling relationship. They may be triggered by everyday events. They may also be awakened when a woman looks at photographs from her childhood, when she remembers family outings, when she draws pictures of her childhood, or through a variety of other memory exploration activities. When those feelings come up, the adult woman has the opportunity to connect with that wounded child and deal with the old hurts inside.

Janice, for example, was a frustrated overachiever. A professional woman, she appeared to have everything she could want—a good paying part-time job, a loving husband, two adorable children, no weight problems, and involvement in a great church. Yet she sought counseling because of depression and anxiety. No matter what she did for others or what she accomplished, Janice never felt that she did enough. She wasn't happy unless everyone around her was happy, and the tension of trying to please everyone was taking a heavy toll. The headaches that had been a part of her daily life for years were becoming unbearable, but her physician could find nothing wrong with her.

Realizing that she might be a codependent, Janice became involved in a twelve-step group for codependents and an Overcomer's Outreach group that was exclusively women. Through her participation in these groups, she began to realize that she wasn't alone, that others had similar struggles. Within the safety of those who accepted her fully, she connected with the pain in her own heart. As her tears flowed, she remembered being a little girl and trying so hard to please her father. Yet nothing she did softened his criticism and judgment of her. Even though her father was now very supportive of her, she couldn't silence his negative, critical voice from her childhood that she heard over and over again inside. With the shame of that critical voice ringing in her ears, she was unable to set boundaries or know when to stop caring for others.

By connecting with the feelings of the wounded child inside, Janice, as an adult, was able to direct the feelings of shame and pain back to her earthly father, where they belonged. She was able to share her deep feelings of shame with her support group. When shame is brought into the open, it loses its power. Set free from the controlling power of shame in her life, Janice began to set boundaries in her relationships. She no longer tried to do everything and please everyone. She was no longer robbed of the joy of her accomplishments, and suffered fewer and fewer headaches. She began to grow into the person God had created her to be.

There is yet another connection that is very important in the recovery process. That is a connection with the heavenly Father. The process of spiritual healing, or growth in relationship with the heavenly Father, is where a woman finds ultimate healing for the father wound.

For some women, the wounds in their relationship with their earthly fathers are so hurtful that they suffer a greatly diminished relationship with God the Father. Some women find it difficult to even read the Bible, hear Christian music, or go to church. This is perhaps the greatest tragedy of the father wound, because the heavenly Father is the perfect Father. He never shames. He always loves. He never rages. He always comforts. And no matter how far away from Him we may feel, He is much closer than we can ever imagine.

I have found that as a woman progresses in the healing process, her heart becomes more open to the loving touch of the heavenly Father. At times, when a woman connects with the painful feelings of her inner child, I will ask her to imagine Jesus standing beside her. I will have her ask Jesus to be her Daddy, to love and protect her in whatever pain she suffers. When that happens, nothing can stop the tears. A very deep and precious healing takes place in the heart of a woman when she connects on a feeling level with the reality of her loving, heavenly Father.

Questions

1. In what ways, healthy or unhealthy, have you dealt with the pain of your past?

2. At what point in your life did you feel compelled to start your journey toward healing? What factors and feelings helped you choose to heal?

3. If you have not yet begun this journey, what is holding you back? What are your fears? What is the next step toward healing?

4. What are your support systems? How can you use those healing connections more effectively?

5. God wants healing in your life. Pray that His loving presence will be real to you in the days ahead.

CHAPTER 9

Forgiving Dad

How a daughter walks through the process of restoring an emotional and spiritual connection with her father.

For years Carole had struggled with anxiety and depression. Her husband, Jim, was an alcoholic and sex addict. He was a horror to live with, but he managed to keep his job and put up a good front. One reason he was able to keep up a good front is because Carole did everything for him. He never had to face the consequences of his actions. Carole made it work no matter what, but the strain was pushing her to the breaking point. Something had to change.

Carole desperately needed support in her life, but she wasn't getting it at her church and, because of the struggles at home, found it difficult to consistently participate in a support group. Because she was ashamed of what was happening in her marriage, Carole would not share her struggles with her friends or the women in her Bible study group. During one of our counseling sessions I said, "Carole, you cannot make changes in your life without some kind of support. Would you want your father to come to a session with you so he could understand what is happening in your life? I suspect that he would want to help you."

"Oh no," she replied. "I could never do that. He believes that you stick with a marriage no matter what. If he knew the truth, he would be so disappointed in me."

"Even so, I think it would be worth a try," I answered. "If it doesn't work, it doesn't work. You have no support now, and given your situation he's the most likely source of support you have. You really have nothing to lose."

Several sessions later, Carole brought her father with her. Walking into a counselor's office for the first time can be a scary thing for a sixty-year-old man, so he felt uncomfortable and at first was mildly defensive. I explained that is was important for a father to build an emotional and spiritual bridge to his daughter, and he looked at me uncertainly. When I added that it is difficult for fathers to do this because most men haven't had such a connection with their fathers, I saw a tear in the corner of his eye. He wasn't about to let his feelings loose, however.

Next I explained that Carole was going through a very difficult time in her life and that she needed a close relationship with him in which she could count on his understanding and support. I asked him to listen to her without interrupting as she explained her situation to him.

For the first time, Carole told her father what life with Jim was like. She told him about Jim's alcoholism and sexual addiction. She described how Jim would scream at *her and the children. As she talked about the daily battles and hurts, tears came into her father's eyes. Carole could see that he felt her pain. When she finished, he said, "I'm sorry that you have had to go through this. I will do anything I can to help you. Even if you feel that you need to move out, I will help you."*

During the months that followed, Carole's father kept in touch with her regularly. He listened to her when she told him how she was doing. He affirmed her decision to seek counseling and the changes she was trying to bring about in her marriage. Carole was no longer emotionally alone in the battles she fought. She had the strength and support of her father standing behind her. Once she had acceptance from her father, she had the courage to begin attending a support group. Gradually she developed better boundaries with her husband, and when their home life reached a crisis point she was able to tell her husband that he needed to get treatment or she would leave him.

Taking that firm stand with her husband was a miraculous step for Carole. She had been raised in a church where women were taught to submit to their husbands without exception. For years Carole had tried to ignore the fact that no amount of submission to her husband's destructive behavior would end the pain she and her children experienced in their home. She was so ashamed of what she thought was her failure to change her husband by her submission that she was even afraid to share the truth about her marriage with her father. Yet when she reached out to her father, he responded with his heart, and the emotional and spiritual bond between them began to be restored. Because her father showed his love for her by connecting with her on an emotional level and supporting her as she walked through the difficulties of her life, she was released from her shame and became empowered to continue healing.

Although it is the father's responsibility to build an emotional and spiritual bridge to his daughter, the reality is that many fathers are unaware of this need in their daughters' lives. Even if they are aware of the need, most fathers have not experienced this kind of connection with their fathers and have few clues as to how to go about touching the heart of a daughter. A daughter who is in recovery, however, becomes connected with her feelings and becomes aware of her desire and need for an emotional bond with her father. It naturally follows that she will want to reach out to her father and establish an emotional and spiritual bond with him. Although it is preferable for the father to seek to build this bond, it is possible, as Carole discovered, for the daughter to initiate the process.

Reaching Out Toward Dad

Before an adult daughter can reach out to her father, she has to let go of her expectations for their relationship. She has to let go of the father she never had, as well as the father she may never have. If there is no emotional bond between them to begin with, it is unwise for her to assume that she can have a serious talk with her father and immediately have the kind of relationship she desires. The fact is, no matter how pleasant or well intentioned her father may be, he may not be capable of the kind of relationship she wants. So, just as there is risk in the recovery process, there is a risk in seeking to reestablish a connection with the father. Although giving up expectations of a wonderful relationship is not easy, a woman must realize that reaching out toward her father is something she needs and desires to do regardless of the outcome.

Since this is no easy thing to do, I generally don't recommend that a woman try to establish an emotional and spiritual connection with her father unless she has a strong recovery underway. A woman who seeks to connect with her father on a feeling level needs to have strong boundaries and ample support. This gives her strength to address the issues that stand between her and her father. In fact, with the women I have counseled, it isn't unusual for a woman to have her whole recovery group praying for her at the exact time she talks with her father.

With a background of recovery and support, a woman can take a variety of approaches to connect with her father. Some women, like Carole, will ask their fathers to join them in counseling. Others will write a letter to their fathers and then meet to talk about it. Still others will write a letter and then read it to their fathers, asking that their fathers refrain from comment until the whole letter is read.

If the daughter is very fortunate, her father will immediately connect with what she is saying, but this doesn't normally happen. In most cases a father will be somewhat defensive. It is important for the daughter to realize why this happens. If her father is like most, he hasn't had an emotional bond with his father and is unaware that there is something missing in the relationship with his daughter. He thinks that because he is proud of her and has given her an education and a good start in life, he has done a great job. It may be difficult for him to understand why she is upset or why she wants something more from him when he thinks he has already given her more than enough. It is not easy for any of us to face our shortcomings, especially when we have done the best we knew how. So defensiveness or anger is a fairly normal response.

In order to handle this kind of response, the daughter needs to have strong enough boundaries so that she doesn't take his defensiveness personally. She has to remember that his lack of awareness or understanding isn't her fault.

It isn't a problem she has to fix. It is her father's problem and responsibility. She also needs to recognize that, just as recovery and healing take place over time, reconnecting with her father takes place over time.

Reconnecting with the father becomes even more difficult if the father is active in his addiction—alcohol, work, food, sex, or whatever he does to alter his moods. A daughter must be conscious of the reality of those addictions and how they affect the interaction between her and her father. She must realize that as long as the addiction is in force, her father isn't fully capable of developing the relationship she desires. So she must be strong enough to sustain an extended "on again, off again" relationship. If this is the situation in which she finds herself, it is very important that she have strong support to keep her own recovery on track. Although it doesn't happen frequently, some daughters in this situation have been able to muster support from other family members and participate in an intervention to motivate the father to seek sobriety.

Finally, a daughter who seeks to establish an emotional bond with her father must realize that her ongoing recovery is a significant part of the reconnecting process. As she becomes healthier and stronger, it becomes increasingly difficult for her father to maintain the status quo. He will have to change as his daughter changes. Sooner or later he will realize that change is necessary if he is going to have a meaningful relationship with his daughter. If he doesn't change, loneliness is his option.

When a Daughter Has Been a Victim of Abuse

A woman who has been abused suffers a tremendous wound in her relationship with her father. Tragically, this is true even when her father is not the perpetrator. Abuse from any source causes the daughter to feel unprotected, and this is a wound in her relationship with her father. Abuse damages the father-daughter relationship in such a way that both father and daughter lose out. The abuser in essence becomes part of the relationship, standing between the father and daughter. In most cases, the father doesn't even know the abuse has happened, yet he is the one who must deal with the damage of that abuse in his relationship with his daughter.

When a girl is abused by another man, she feels shame, and those feelings dictate her relationships. The wounded part of her either distances from her father because all men seem dangerous and scary, or the wounded part of her becomes overly enmeshed with her father because she desperately wants to know that he still loves her. Both of these responses lead to further damage in the relationship.

If the daughter withdraws, the father may not even notice the change. If he does notice, he may not have any idea how to reestablish an emotional bond. The sad truth is, unless he knows the abuse has occurred, he is clueless as to how to rebuild an emotional bridge to his daughter. As time goes on, he and his daughter will grow further and further apart because of the third party's influence on the relationship.

If the daughter takes the other approach and pursues inappropriate intimacy with her father, the father-daughter relationship suffers damage in other ways. A daughter who takes this approach may be extremely needy and physical with her father, as if boundaries don't exist. She may want to be held all the time. She may hug and kiss her father inappropriately. Understandably, a father who seeks to maintain appropriate boundaries wants no part of this. He may push his daughter away or avoid physical contact with her. This response adds further confusion and hurt to the relationship and leaves the daughter with weak, underdeveloped boundaries that will fail under pressure.

In both scenarios, the father-daughter relationship usually becomes increasingly stressful, even bizarre. In order for the relationship to change, the truth concerning the abuse has to be made known. Yet it takes a tremendous amount of courage for a daughter to tell her father and mother what has happened to her. She doesn't know beforehand what her father's response will be, so support is essential for her to be able to reveal this dark secret. Many times women I have counseled will have their fathers come into my office, where they are not alone and where they feel a sense of safety, when they break the news of abuse.

A father's response to learning about the abuse his daughter has suffered is powerful. Many times he will weep and weep because what has happened stirs up such strong feelings within him. He may feel so much rage that he wants to kill the guy who abused his daughter. He may be overcome with guilt and shame because he wasn't able to protect his daughter from the abuse. He may feel overwhelmed by the realization of what happened and suddenly understand why the relationship has been so confusing. As difficult as it is to deal with such powerful emotions, it is a good thing that the father feels them because it helps the daughter know that what happened to her is real. It also helps her to know that her father has deep love and compassion for her.

As in all attempts to reconnect with the father, a daughter who reveals a history of abuse faces significant risk in the process. Abuse results in damaged boundaries. When an abused daughter witnesses the pain her father feels because of the abuse, she will often feel that she has caused his pain. She will be tempted to keep silent because she doesn't want to hurt him. This is why it is important for a daughter in this situation to have a solid recovery and adequate support. She has to have enough strength so that she doesn't take on the burden of her father's pain. It is not her responsibility to do anything to lessen what he is feeling. He has to find his own way through it.

Once the abuse has been exposed, the third party, although not eliminated, is at least a known entity. This opens the door for rebuilding the father-daughter relationship. The father and daughter who have dealt with the reality of abuse have already handled a difficult issue. If the father responds to his daughter's pain on a feeling level, the bond between them is already strengthened. They may well make good progress in addressing the other issues in their relationship.

When Dad Isn't Safe

Of course, there are times when the perpetrator of abuse is not a third party, but is the woman's father. Even when a woman has been abused by her father, the hunger for an emotional and spiritual bond with him is often so great that she will want to try to establish such a connection with him. This is an extremely risky step to take, one that a woman should not even consider unless she has "major league support."

Trying to touch the feeling level of an abusive father is a monumental task. There are incredibly difficult obstacles to work through. If the father is still active in his addictions, the daughter has to get through the addictions in order to connect with her father. If she gets through the addictions and actually has an interaction with her father, she will run into a solid wall of denial. A perpetrator has to have a tremendous amount of denial to commit abuse in the first place, and denial becomes more deeply entrenched as time passes. In addition to her father's denial, the daughter also has to confront the denial of others in relationship to him.

This may include the denial of a codependent wife, as well as that of siblings, family friends, and even his church. Often when there is abuse, strong denial, and active addiction, the father is disconnected from his own feelings; he may even be a multiple personality. It is as if one part of him lives in California and another part lives in Ecuador!

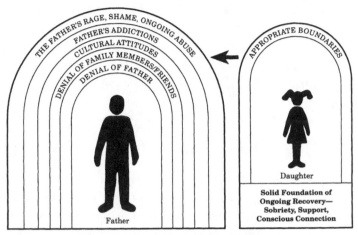

Reconnecting with an Abusive Father

A daughter has to break through an incredibly strong wall to reach the heart of an abusive father. This is why she must have a strong recovery program underway.

As long as the father is disconnected from the feeling part of himself, he cannot connect with his daughter on a feeling level. All of these obstacles have to be broken down before the daughter can begin to make the connection she desires to make. This is why an unshakable recovery program and strong support are absolutely necessary before a woman even considers reaching out to an abusive father.

In addition to her ongoing recovery and support, it is also wise for a woman who desires to make a connection with an abusive father to involve a third person, such as a pastor or therapist, in the process. One important function of the third party is to assess whether or not the father is an emotional killer. An emotional killer is usually a person who has also been abused and is disconnected from his feelings. The devastating thing about an emotional killer is that there is no consistent reality in a relationship with this person. A daughter may have a confrontation in which her father will admit the abuse, but the next day or an hour later, he will absolutely deny it.

An emotional killer has industrial-strength denial! His denial is so powerful that he truly believes the abuse, which he may even have admitted to previously, never happened. The possibility of connecting with a father who is an emotional killer is remote.

It is difficult for some people to realize that denial can be this powerful, but consider for a moment how our memory works. Most people can recall events that happened fifteen, twenty, or thirty years ago and wonder if they really happened just as they remember. If a person experienced those events with another person and that person confirms the memory, the memory can become clearer and more real. A certain amount of uncertainty or fuzziness of memory is a fact of normal recall. When we factor in that a perpetrator of abuse is dealing with memories of sick, horrible, shame-filled, depraved events, it isn't difficult to see how the mind naturally moves toward denial or an inability to recall the event.

When we realize what is taking place in the mind and feelings of an emotional killer, we gain a great respect for what takes place in twelve-step groups. When a person makes a lifetime commitment to recovery and regularly participates in twelve-step meetings, a more consistent reality results. A person involved in twelve-step work knows that, left to his or her own devices, trouble will result. Within the twelve-step support system, however, the person is able to expose the insanity of his or her own thinking—the deceit, lies, manipulation, and control—without receiving condemnation and can begin to deal with it. I am in no way implying that all people who are involved in twelve-step groups are emotional killers, but if this kind of support and work is necessary to help an alcoholic deal with reality, one can only imagine how necessary it is in helping an emotional killer deal with reality.

I explain this in order to show how unlikely it is for a daughter to connect with an abusive father—especially an emotional killer—who is not in recovery. In most cases, powerful outside forces must be at work to pressure an emotional killer to change. These might come through a dramatic spiritual experience or a family intervention, but even then it is up to the individual to sustain the recovery.

During twenty years of counseling, I have seen perhaps half a dozen instances in which a daughter connected with an abusive father. In each case, massive intervention was required. Even such intervention often isn't sufficient to hold the person accountable. The only protection against an abusive father who will not remain in recovery is to have solid, impermeable boundaries.

To understand what kind of intervention and external force is required to bring about change in an emotional killer, consider what typically happens when I counsel a teenager who has suffered abuse from her father. Once the abuse is revealed, the legal and criminal justice system comes into play. The father can't easily brush off the forces that demand accountability. He faces arrest. He has to go to court. He faces emotional and physical separation from his family. His actions become public knowledge. He may be forced to undergo counseling. He may lose his job and even go to jail. A father in this position has no escape, so he is usually motivated to do whatever he can to prove that he really is a good guy. When all of these forces are applied, there is a higher chance of a sustained recovery.

When a daughter has a father who is too sick to have a relationship with, she experiences a real emptiness. Her best option is to continue with her own recovery and support. This is important so that her need for a father does not deceive her into believing that her father is less dangerous than he is. No one can replace a father, but other relationships, including a woman's relationship with God the Father, can do much to fill her emptiness. Although a daughter's options for restoring a bond with an abusive father are very limited, she can continue to heal and forgive. She can continue to maintain strong boundaries with her father so that she is not vulnerable to further abuse.

When It's Time to Forgive

There comes a time in a woman's journey toward healing when forgiveness plays a tremendously important role in her relationship with her father. For some women who have been deeply wounded through the father-daughter relationship, even the mention of forgiveness can produce a powerful emotional reaction. Forgiveness is never easy, and in some cases it seems impossible. Yet forgiveness, especially for Christian women who have experienced unconditional forgiveness from God the Father, has its place.

Unfortunately, the meaning and role of forgiveness has all too often been misunderstood. Some people consider forgiveness to be the same as condoning a wrong action. Others view forgiveness as a gift to the perpetrator and further punishment for the victim. Still others think of forgiveness as an open invitation for future abuse. And within some Christian circles, forgiveness often becomes a vehicle of shame rather than the liberating force God intended it to be. Rather than describing forgiveness, these views distort forgiveness. Allow me to explain what I mean.

Forgiveness is a divine gift. We have all wronged God and

deserve to suffer the consequences of our sin. However, when we confess our sins to God, He promises to forgive those sins and to cleanse us from all unrighteousness.[1] The reason God can offer forgiveness to us freely is because Christ has already paid the consequences for our sins through His sacrificial death on the cross. Since Christ has already paid the consequences, all that is necessary for us to do to receive God's forgiveness is to confess our sins.

We get into trouble, however, when we apply the divine model for forgiveness to earthly relationships. Just as there are consequences of sin, there are consequences when a wound is suffered. No one who has major surgery goes out and engages in three hours of aerobics the same day. He or she must allow the surgical wounds to heal. In a similar way, emotional and spiritual wounds require time to heal. Forgiveness is a part of the healing process, but it is no substitute for healing.

We are fortunate that Jesus paid the consequences for our sins and opened the way for our wounded relationship with our heavenly Father to be healed through our humble confession. In our earthly relationships, however, the consequences are not automatically paid and the wounds are not automatically healed. It takes time for healing and forgiveness to take place. All too often we shame those who have been wounded through a relationship when we demand forgiveness and assume that healing instantly follows. What we ask is not humanly possible.

Forgiveness and healing of human relationships are related, but separate, issues. In order to understand the difference between forgiveness and healing, let's consider the following common misconceptions about forgiveness:

- Forgiveness = Trust
- Forgiveness = No Consequences, No Boundaries

- Forgiveness = No Change in Behavior or Mention of the Past

Misconception #1: Forgiveness = Trust. The story about Leo the Lion illustrates this misconception well. Leo was the star attraction of the circus. Every night his trainer would put him through his paces and end the act by shaking hands with Leo. One night, however, Leo was a bit hungry. He got grumpy when he was hungry, and by the end of his act he let his anger get the best of him. Instead of shaking the trainer's hand, he took a swipe at her arm and lacerated it badly.

After the show, Leo said he was sorry for hurting his trainer, and the trainer forgave him. But the next night, the trainer didn't attempt to shake Leo's hand. "What's wrong with you?" Leo snarled. "I said I was sorry. Aren't you going to forgive me?"

"I have forgiven you," the trainer said. "I'm just not ready to risk shaking your paw. I'm going to make sure you have better control of your anger before I take that risk again."

With an angry roar, Leo took another swipe at his trainer. But this time his trainer was far enough away to avoid injury!

Many of us are a bit like Leo. When we wrong others, we want forgiveness. We also want the relationship to be restored as soon as possible (which really means instantly). We then are upset if trust isn't restored immediately following our apology.

Trust, however, is a result of time and experience, not a result of forgiveness. Trust grows out of the spiritual and emotional healing process. For some wounds, trust is restored rather quickly. For deeper wounds, the restoration of trust takes longer. A father who has wounded his daughter cannot expect the restoration of trust to occur on his timetable. The restoration of trust is in his daughter's hands, a fact that can be difficult for him to accept.

Although a father cannot control the rebuilding of trust, he can control his behavior. And, as Leo the Lion discovered, his behavior strongly influences his daughter's ability to trust him. A father (such as the emotional killer described earlier) who chooses to deny or minimize the impact of his behavior and continues to engage in behavior that wounds his daughter is not trustworthy. His daughter can forgive him so that her feelings of hurt, anger, fear, or resentment do not harm her, but she would be foolish to trust him. For her own protection, she must maintain strong boundaries with him.

Of course, not all fathers are stuck in denial. A father who has discovered the depth of his own wounds and has felt how he has wounded his daughter often makes a commitment to his own healing and growth. Such a father is certainly not perfect, but he will change. In time, his daughter can feel safe with him. She will realize that he is not the father he used to be, and her trust in him can grow.

Misconception #2: Forgiveness = No Consequences, No Boundaries. One consequence of wounding is that healing needs to take place. Although forgiveness promotes healing, no amount of forgiveness can eliminate the need to heal or the time required to heal. A daughter whose wounds are raw and who feels fragile and vulnerable may need to distance herself from her father for a season while her trust rebuilds. The daughter of an actively addicted or co-dependent father may need to set boundaries to protect herself (and perhaps her children) from the father. These consequences are not comfortable or enjoyable, but they are a necessary part of the healing process. The wise father who finds himself in this situation will continue to grow spiritually and emotionally, while he prayerfully waits through his daughter's healing process.

Dorothy and her father had to address this misconception. Although Dorothy's father was successful at work and a recognized leader at church, he was a closet alcoholic. Her mother was a first-class codependent who denied that her husband even had a problem. Dorothy had been in recovery for some time and had made good progress in healing from the hurt, anger, and shame of the double-standard household in which she grew up. She had pulled away from her parents early in her recovery and one day felt strong enough to approach her father and talk to him about what had been happening in her life.

"Dad," she said when they were alone, "I haven't been by to see you and Mom for a long time, and you have no idea why I have pulled away from you. I think it is time you know that I have always been afraid of you when you drink. I was afraid of you when I was a little girl, and more recently I have been angry with you because of your drinking. I can now forgive you for the past, and I ask you to forgive me for my anger. It was wrong for me to hold that against you for so long."

Her words touched her father deeply. "It's a relief to know why you haven't come by to see us. Thank you for forgiving me, and of course I forgive you. When will you drop by again? Could the kids spend a weekend with us soon?"

"I would like to do that Dad, and this is hard for me to say, but my children will not be with you unless I am present," Dorothy said calmly. She then took a deep breath and added, "You also need to know that if you are ever drunk when we come to see you, or if you start drinking while we are visiting, we will leave immediately."

Instantly her father's face turned red. "How can you say

you are a Christian? You haven't forgiven me! Forgiven means forgotten!"

"Dad, I have forgiven you," Dorothy repeated. "I also know that you are not the same person when you drink as you are when you are sober. I can choose, for me and for my children, not to be around you if you choose to drink."

Dorothy left her parents' house that day with her father angry at her and her mother in tears. For two months she had no contact with her parents, then her mother called and asked if they could talk. Dorothy agreed, and when they met she asked her mother's forgiveness for the anger and resentment she had harbored against her.

By that time, Dorothy had realized that her anger toward her parents had served as a boundary to keep her safe. Yet boundaries of anger and resentment take a terrible toll on a person. For Dorothy, that toll had meant problems in her marriage, chronic headaches, and bouts with depression. Through counseling and her support group, Dorothy was learning how to set boundaries without being angry. She was learning that respect for personal boundaries is one of the characteristics of a healthy relationship. She was learning that forgiving her parents did not mean she was unable to maintain protective boundaries in the relationship or to set consequences for violations of those boundaries.

When Dorothy met with her mother, they talked about the family and her father's alcoholism. As they talked, her mother began to realize that her denial was part of the problem. As a result of their conversation, Dorothy's mother began attending Al-Anon meetings with her daughter. In time, her mother's recovery from codependency enabled the family to do an intervention on her father that initiated his recovery from alcoholism. An intervention involves setting firm boundaries that are backed by serious consequences. It is not an easy action to take. In this case, as in many others, setting firm boundaries that carry stiff consequences was a necessary part of the healing of family relationships.

The change in her parents' behavior brought new consequences to the family. Dorothy, her husband, and her children could at last enjoy the kind of relationship with her parents that they had long desired. Consequences and boundaries, rather than being the opposite of forgiveness, enable forgiveness and healing to take place.

Misconception #3: Forgiveness = No Change in Behavior or Mention of the Past. It is unfortunate, but the word *forgiveness* is often used like a steamroller to cover up a multitude of issues. In practical terms, forgiveness often means, "Let's just go on from here as if this never happened. We're not going to talk about dirty laundry. What's in the past is in the past." The problem with this approach is two-fold: the past is not dealt with, and there is no requirement for a change in behavior.

This is not true forgiveness. It is nothing short of denial. If healing of the relationship is to occur, behavior must change *and* the past cannot be left unanswered. To understand this, let's consider the dynamics of Elizabeth's relationship with her father, Bill.

Bill was a work addict and an alcoholic, but a dramatic change occurred when Elizabeth was twelve years old. Bill was arrested for driving under the influence of alcohol. While he sat in jail, he realized that his life was completely out of control. At that time, he asked Jesus to forgive him and made a commitment to change his life. When he was released from jail, his good friend who had been sharing Christ with him steered him to a church that was supportive of recovery and urged him to participate in Alcoholics Anonymous and Overcomers Outreach meetings. Bill was faithful in growing in his newfound faith and his commitment to sobriety. As he worked the twelve steps, he made amends to his wife and daughter.

Despite these changes, all was not well at home. When Elizabeth was fourteen years old, she started expressing great anger and resentment toward her father. She had seen the change in her father and knew that he was sincere in his efforts to make amends, but this only made her feel worse. *What kind of a daughter am I,* she thought, *to be so angry at a father who is so much better than he used to be?* Bill was wise enough to suspect that her anger was rooted in his years of alcoholism, so he suggested that they go to counseling together.

Through counseling Elizabeth learned to recognize and verbalize her feelings. She expressed her anger and disappointment at the times he had broken promises to attend her soccer games because he forgot or was too hung over to come. Through many tears, she talked about her fears when Bill would drink and fight with her mother. She talked about how scared she was when he would leave the house in a rage and drive away fast—how she was afraid that he would never come home and at the same time was afraid that he would come home.

When she finished talking, Bill was crying, too. "I'm so sorry," he said. "I am sorry my actions hurt you so deeply. I hope the day will come when you will be able to forgive me for what I have done." Bill offered no explanation, no defense. He simply acknowledged that he was guilty as charged.

For several minutes, Elizabeth sobbed deeply. I then asked her if she would like her father to sit next to her and hold her.

"No," she said. "I can't trust him yet."

"That's okay," Bill said. "I have hurt you deeply. When you are ready, I will be here for you."

When Bill allowed Elizabeth to keep her distance, she

immediately felt safer with him. She could feel that he respected her needs and her pain. "You can sit next to me if you would like," she added.

When Bill sat down near her, Elizabeth began to cry again. In time, she allowed him to hold and comfort her. In time, she was able to forgive him for the wounds of the past. This emotional healing between father and daughter would not have happened if the wounds of the past had not been addressed, or if Bill's behavior had not changed.

Repentance and Forgiveness in Healthy Relationships

The Bible has a great deal to say about relationships—relationships between all of humanity and God, relationships between parents and children, relationships between husbands and wives, and relationships between believers. It also has much to say about repentance and forgiveness. I don't believe this is mere coincidence. God knows that repentance and forgiveness play an ongoing role in all human relationships, so He gives us as much wisdom in these areas as possible. With that understanding, notice what Jesus says about repentance and forgiveness:

So watch yourselves. If your brother sins, rebuke him, and if he repents, forgive him. If he sins against you seven times in a day, and seven times comes back to you and says, I repent, forgive him.[2]

- I believe Jesus is warning us to be aware of what is happening in our relationships and to take appropriate action when we are wronged. This means several things:
- If someone wrongs us, we are to bring it out in the

open and talk about it. We aren't to ignore it or sweep it under the rug.

- If the person repents, which means acknowledging the wrong and having a change of heart and behavior, we must forgive the person.
- Even if the person repeats the same wrong, we are to forgive when repentance is offered.

Our relationships are important, and repentance and forgiveness are necessary ingredients of healthy relationships. When Peter asked Jesus if he should forgive his brother as many as seven times, Jesus answered, "Not seven, but seventy-seven times."[3] It is easy for us to be thankful that God is always forgiving, but this degree of forgiveness on the human level may seem like a steep bill for us to fill. If we equate forgiveness with the misconceptions that it means immediate trust, no consequences, no boundaries, no change in behavior, and no mention of the past, then Jesus' answer is impossible! But when we strip away the misconceptions, we realize it is possible to forgive.

When we forgive, we release the anger, resentment, fear, and worry we have attached to the wrongs committed against us. Forgiveness in no way justifies the wrong committed, but it promotes healing in the heart of the person who has been wronged. In fact, some medical doctors cite a tendency to hold resentment and a marked inability to forgive as part of the process through which some people develop serious illnesses.[4] Robin Casarjian, a therapist who has written extensively about forgiveness, summarizes the healing aspect of forgiveness well:

> So often when people think about forgiveness they think about what it's going to do for someone else. . . . They say, "I'm not going to forgive them, after what they did," as if forgiving them would be doing the other person a favor.

What they don't realize is that forgiveness is really an act of self-interest. We're doing ourselves a favor, because we become free to have a more peaceful life—we free ourselves from being emotional victims of others.[5]

Forgiveness truly does bring freedom. When we discover what forgiveness is and how boundaries help forgiveness occur, we realize that it is possible to forgive seventy-seven times as a person learns how to change emotionally destructive behaviors. We see that it is possible to clearly express our feelings, to maintain firm boundaries, *and* to forgive. We find that it is possible to discuss the old wounds so that repentance and forgiveness for the past may clear the slate for an ongoing relationship. We understand that it is possible to forgive while we grow toward trust. We learn that it is possible to forgive without exposing ourselves to further mistreatment. Genuine forgiveness does much to accomplish God's healing work in our lives.

Questions

1. Do you feel the need to initiate the bridge-building process with your father?

2. What risks are involved in reaching out to your father?

3. If you are unable to establish a relationship with your father, what positive steps can you take to fill the emptiness his absence leaves?

4. What is your response to the prospect of forgiving your father? How can you begin to see forgiveness as God sees it?

5. Thank God for the process and gift of forgiveness. Pray that He will help you understand what forgiveness means.

CHAPTER 10

When Dad Wants to Connect

How a father can rebuild the emotional and spiritual bridge to his daughter.

Don had been an abusive husband and father. When he finally realized what was happening, he sought help. As he healed from the guilt and shame of his past, he began to realize how much he had hurt his family. His children were now adults, and Don could see how the pain of their growing up years was creating problems in their lives. This was particularly noticeable in his twenty-eight-year-old daughter, Ann, who had a major spending problem.

Although Don could see the pattern of addiction in Ann's behavior, he was, for a long time, powerless to do anything about it. Every time Ann ran out of money, she would call, and he would send her a check. As his recovery deepened, however, Don recognized how his codependent giving was enabling Ann to avoid the issues with which she needed to deal. He also was sufficiently connected to his feelings that he could understand the difference be-

tween giving material things to Ann and giving her himself.

So Don felt ready to take a bold step with his daughter. He met with her and asked forgiveness for his verbal and physical abuse while she was growing up. Ann was touched by his open admission of guilt and lack of defensiveness, but she did not like what followed.

"Ann," Don continued, "I know that you have been deeply wounded by my past behavior. Although I cannot change the past, I can make a difference today. At the present time, your spending is out of control. I have been wrong to have supported this destructive habit for as long as I have. One of the things I must do for you now is to stop giving you money every time you ask for it. This does not mean I love you any less, for I am not abandoning you. I am here for you now more than ever. Whenever you are ready to seek help for your addiction and desire healing from the past, let me know. I will stand by you as you work through these issues and will pay for six months of outpatient counseling."

Adult children can become very angry when the material connection they have with a parent is withdrawn, and Ann was no exception. "You're no better today than you were when I was little," Ann retorted. "Your apology doesn't mean anything to me!"

Unlike his typical response in the past, Don did not react angrily to his daughter's words. He knew beforehand that his action would not be easy for Ann to accept. Before he even approached her, he had talked with me and with his support group about what he planned to do. He also made sure that his boundaries were strong enough so that he did not take her accusation personally.

Months later, Ann called and asked if they could talk. Don, as he had promised, was ready. Ann admitted that she had an alcohol and drug problem and that she was close to losing her job as a result. She asked Don if he could help her get better. He, in turn, helped her find a therapist and stood by her emotionally and financially as she began her recovery. Today they share a strong emotional bond.

Don is a good example of a father who later in life recognized his own pain and deliberately walked the path toward healing and recovery. As his wounds healed and his heart became more alive, he developed a sensitivity to his daughter's wounds. He recognized the flawed relationship he had with her—a relationship that was built on codependency and denial rather than on emotional integrity and trust. Like many fathers who have found healing in their lives, he wanted to make amends for the past and sought to turn the pain of the past relationship into gold.

The Right Starting Point

There is no doubt that it would have been best if Don had built an emotional and spiritual bridge to Ann from the beginning of her life. But when she was young, he was not connected with his pain and feeling life, so he was incapable of reaching out to her. Although her addiction and his codependency made the task more difficult, Don discovered that it is never too late for a father to reach out and start building a bridge to his daughter's heart. The passage of time may make the task harder, but it is not impossible.

No matter what the daughter's age, a father who wants to connect with her must start at the same point: himself. The father's heart and feeling life is the foundation stone of the emotional bridge between father and daughter. A father cannot build a bridge to his daughter if he cannot feel what is in his heart.

A father who has not connected with his feelings, for example, might believe he has a bond with his daughter because he works hard to provide for her, gives her a car, pays for her education, or showers her with gifts. Although these are wonderful expressions of his love, they are not the same as having an emotional and spiritual bond with her. Without an emotional and spiritual connection, the relationship between father and daughter is primarily an illusion. It may appear to be a strong bridge that can weather the most powerful storms life brings, but in reality it is like a paper-mache bridge that will crumble into nothing when put to the test.

A father who is connected with his feelings, on the other hand, feels the weight of his position. He realizes deep in his heart that God has given him a sacred role to fill in nurturing the heart of his daughter. He realizes the impact the feelings of his heart can have on his daughter. He also realizes his imperfections and his tendency toward error and failure. The thought of fulfilling the awesome role of *father* may leave him feeling overwhelmed and powerless. Yet that is not where God leaves him.

As Jesus was dying on the cross, He prayed, "Father, forgive them, for they do not know what they are doing."[1] Fathers today need to remember that prayer. Although directed specifically to the people who crucified Him, it reveals the eternal passion of Jesus' heart: His unfailing compassion for those of us who do wrong without understanding what we are doing. When we fathers do the best we know how to do for our daughters—and still fall short—we can take comfort in God's forgiveness. As a father, I need that. I cringe when I think of the times I have wounded my daughters with shame because I have not faced the shame in my heart. I feel a profound sadness when I consider the times I have wounded my daughters with anger because I was unaware of the anger hidden within me. God's forgiveness is indeed a comfort.

Does God's forgiveness take away my responsibility to do better? No! Do I have to humble myself and make amends to my daughters? Yes! Will it take time for me and my daughters to heal? Definitely! Am I harder on myself than I need to be? Probably! Am I forgiven? Absolutely! I thank God for His forgiveness. It brings healing to my heart and my relationship with Him. The strength of my relationship with Him, my commitment to continued recovery and growth, and the support of other men makes it possible for me to feel and deal with what is in my heart and reach out to the hearts of my daughters.

Connecting with a Daughter's World

The route to a daughter's heart is to learn what is important to her and to share in the discovery of her world. It is, of course, easier for the father to bring the daughter into his world. Although bringing the daughter into his world does have a place in their relationship, it doesn't establish the same bond with her heart as when he shares in the experiences of her world. So we fathers have some learning to do.

In my own situation, I am drawn to physical activity. I feel good when I play basketball, ride a bike, hike into the mountains, or play racquetball. My son and I enjoy these activities together. It is one of the ways in which we connect. My oldest daughter enjoys some of these activities as well, so we have shared them together. I participate in her world when I take her to a Lakers game or when I watch her play basketball.

But I have to connect with my preschool-age daughter in an entirely different way. A walk around the block with my two-year-old does not qualify as aerobic activity. Walking around the block in her world means leaning down to smell a flower, stopping to talk to a dog, sitting down to rest, and answering a thousand questions about the sky and how the clouds got there. If we do anything physical, it is jumping into a puddle or building a dam in the gutter and watching the water build up behind it. You have to admit, this level of participation in a young daughter's world doesn't take a tremendous amount of ability. All it requires is the willingness to make the most of opportunities to share in what she enjoys.

It is important for me to remember that my daughter's world is just as important and valuable in God's eyes as my world is. When she senses my interest and involvement in what is valuable to her, the bond between us deepens. The deep part of her being is nurtured. It's funny, but when I enter her world and share in life as she experiences it, I am nurtured, too. I slow down and rediscover an appreciation for the small delights in life.

Of course, there are other ways a father can connect with his daughter, and those ways change as she matures. Yet it is a challenge for a father to respond to his daughter in a manner that is appropriate for her age and maturity. It is very sad when he responds to his teenage daughter as if she were still six years old. A father needs to recognize his daughter's status as a young woman. He needs to realize that he cannot control her life or protect her from life; she must learn to make her own choices.

Another way to connect with a daughter as she grows up is simply to spend time with her—participating in activities she enjoys, talking with her, asking her about school, listening as she talks about her friends, discovering what she thinks about her world. I have discovered, for example, that one way to nurture Rachel and our relationship is to occasionally take her with me when I travel to speak or conduct a retreat. During these times we have the opportunity to talk together without distractions. We can establish new friendships and enjoy discovering a new part of the country. Rachel has the opportunity to learn more about what I do, and I can answer her questions about my profession. On these trips she also has the opportunity to escape the stresses of her life and spend some quiet time alone. This time of rest and refreshment is important for a teenager who works hard in school, spends many hours babysitting, and has to cope with two younger sisters and an older brother! For all fathers, the challenge in this type of interaction is to be emotionally present—not thinking about all kinds of other things when he is with her.

Another way a father connects with a daughter is to take a genuine interest in activities that interest her. This may mean providing opportunities for her to deepen her experience or explore new possibilities in her areas of interest— whether they be spiritual, physical, creative, or intellectual. The key here is for the father to encourage and support her growth without crossing the line and becoming critical or manipulative.

When a father enters into his daughter's life in these ways, she gains a sense of his affirmation, caring, encouragement, and emotional support. This helps her develop the spiritual and emotional resources she needs to live her life. The result of these connections helps a daughter grow into a woman who has a deep spirituality, strong boundaries, a profound sense of personal identity, and unshakable strength.

Connecting Requires a Concerted Effort

Time is an incredible commodity that we all have in equal portion yet always seem to lack. Thus our choices in how we allocate our time are significant. Nothing happens by accident. A father has to actively set aside time to connect with his daughter. Time that is not planned is time that usually does not occur.

We fathers can make no allocation of time that will guarantee dividends as great as our investment in our daughters. So we cannot afford to approach our time together casually. We need to plan ahead and coordinate our activities with those of our daughters. We need to take note of the time when we or our daughters will be especially busy and make sure we don't neglect spending time together. We need to look for opportunities to connect with our daughters on a regular basis. Perhaps going out for breakfast before school or sharing a meal together between the end of the workday and the start of evening activities would be a good time to connect.

I know this isn't easy to do. I, for example, have to plan retreats and speaking engagements a year in advance, yet I want to be able to attend sporting events and school and church programs that involve my four children. Although we live in the same household, coordinating all of this is a mind-boggling task!

In every family, a father has to work hard to ensure that an emotional bond continues to develop as his daughter grows older. During adolescence, the daughter's life becomes increasingly centered outside the home, so she is often less available to the father. So he must dedicate an increasing amount of effort to maintain an emotional and spiritual bond between them. The task becomes even more difficult when a family also faces the separation of divorce.

Connecting After Divorce

When parents divorce, the contact between father and daughter is usually greatly reduced. Although the daughter may live with the father in some cases, the father and daughter most often cease to live in the same house. They may be together as often as every weekend or as little as one or two weeks out of the year. When a daughter has infrequent contact with her father, she usually learns one of two things: "Do not expect anything from men," or, "Always expect Disneyland."

Neither of these options is nurturing to the daughter. Neither promotes a deep sense of her own identity and worth —to her father, God, or anyone else. Neither challenges her to deal with life in a realistic way. Neither teaches her how to accept responsibility and establish appropriate boundaries. Neither builds up her feminine strength.

When she has insufficient contact with her father, a daughter feels abandoned. She may be so hungry inside for a father that if a guy shows her any attention, she wants to be with him all the time. She may also become very enmeshed with his family—not necessarily the specific guy and his family, but the idea of belonging to a family. On the other hand, if the father indulges his daughter every time they are together and spends the whole time playing or buying things for her, she becomes used to having nothing but ice cream. She then may expect other men to treat her royally and become extremely bored and depressed about ordinary living.

A father who finds himself in the position of being the custodial parent may have the opportunity to spend more time with his daughter and strengthen the bond between them, but he has other concerns to guard against. He must realize that he cannot be everything for his daughter and she cannot be everything for him. No matter how hard he tries, he cannot meet all of his daughter's needs. No matter how much she may want to help him, he cannot allow her to meet all of his needs. He will need the support of others, both for himself and for his daughter, if he is to parent her effectively.

A custodial father must be very careful that the bond

between him and his daughter does not turn into emotional incest. Although it is appropriate for her to help maintain the household, he needs to ensure that she does not carry the responsibility for these tasks. He should not allow her to take on the role of wife—caring for his clothes, preparing his meals, doing the shopping, and the like. If the father allows his daughter to become a surrogate wife in this sense, he will have to go through another divorce if he ever decides to remarry. This time he will have to divorce his daughter. She will understand this second divorce even less than the first.

Emotional incest can also be difficult to guard against because it is so frequently rewarded. The father may reward the daughter for her help. Relatives or family friends may say things like, "Oh, you are such a fine young woman because you take such good care of your dad! What would he do without you?" This kind of talk sounds nice on the surface, but it is destructive rather than nurturing to the daughter.

A custodial father whose daughter has a limited relationship with her mother must also ensure that his daughter has some kind of consistent relationship with older women. This mentoring relationship may be with a grandmother, aunt, family friend, or woman in the church—any trustworthy woman who will commit to a consistent relationship with the daughter over a period of time. This relationship becomes essential as the daughter makes the transition from child to young woman. Fathers are not equipped to handle some aspects of this transition. The wise father will ensure that trustworthy women are available to mentor his daughter through this transition. These mentoring relationships will take some of the pressure off the father-daughter relationship so that the father can continue to nurture the daughter in the way only he can.

Connecting with an Adult Daughter

Fathers need to realize that fathering doesn't end when a daughter graduates from school, moves out of the home, or marries. I have yet to hear an adult woman say that her father calls her too much or is too supportive of her. No matter what her age, the little girl inside still desires affirmation, understanding, and nurturing from her father. She still wants to know that he is proud of the woman she has become. She still wants the opportunity to share some of her joys, sorrows, frustrations, fears, and worries with him.

Because of this need, adult women are still wounded when their fathers are not emotionally responsive to them. They still have grand hopes that their fathers will—perhaps today—respond differently. Shortly after Debra miscarried, for example, her father called. In tears, she told him what had happened and that she was scheduled for a D and C. "Oh," her father said, "can I talk with Bob [her husband]?" Debra was crushed. Her father had responded to her pain as if she had told him they were having a new roof put on the house. Not only did she have to deal with the loss of her baby, her grief was compounded by her father's present insensitivity and all of the wounds she had suffered through his lack of emotional responsiveness in the past. Understandably, Debra felt very weak and alone at that point in time.

Even a father who is capable of having an emotionally connected relationship with his daughter must realize that their relationship changes as his daughter moves into adulthood. He can't play by the old rules. He has to move away from an active role of setting limits and intervening in her life to that of listening, supporting, and encouraging her as an independent adult. He must recognize that his daughter has her own ideas, opinions, and feelings. He must realize that she will spend her lifetime growing and maturing, which includes making mistakes. Although he can no longer prevent her from making mistakes, his support can make it much easier for her to recover from them.

When an adult daughter has a strong emotional and spiritual bond with her father, she gains a tremendous sense of security that enables her to handle the risks of life. It may seem surprising, but the father actually has to *do* very little to instill this sense of security; it is almost as if his faithful presence in her life is enough. The daughter knows she has someone to turn to in times of trouble, someone who can help her walk through the scary times. Whether she starts a business, takes a new job, or weathers a difficult time in her marriage, she has confidence that her father believes in her and accepts her no matter what the outcome. This is a tremendous gift that empowers her to fulfill her potential. It is the kind of fathering that Mordecai gave to Esther.

Rebuilding the Bond

It is very special when a father realizes what has been lost in his relationship with his daughter and seeks to establish an emotional and spiritual bond with her. When I talk to the adult daughters of such fathers, they clearly have positive feelings about their relationship with their fathers. A daughter is strengthened and empowered when her father calls her at work, takes her out to lunch, offers to entertain the kids for a bit, or simply shows genuine interest in the person she has become and the world in which she lives.

Tom, for example, is in his fifties and has been in recovery for several years. When he connected with his own woundedness in his relationship with his father, he realized what he was missing in his relationship with his adult daughter. He wanted his relationship with her to be better, and today it is. She welcomes the one or two telephone calls he makes to her office every week. They don't talk long, but he asks how her work is going and listens as she shares what she is feeling. For a few minutes every week, he connects with her world.

A father must realize, however, that the process of reconnecting with an adult daughter is not a rose-lined path. He has to be willing to initiate a relationship without expectations. He must accept the level of relationship that his daughter is willing and able to give. This may mean he will have to try, try, and try again without becoming frustrated by his daughter's possible anger, resentment, or coldness. A father who wants to connect with his daughter can't give up after only one, two, or even three tries.

Tom discovered this through firsthand experience. When he started calling his daughter, she seemed to enjoy it, but after a few weeks she became a bit cold toward him. Not knowing what to do, Tom was tempted to give up. *Well*, he thought, *she just doesn't want much of a relationship with me anyway.* So he asked me what to do.

"Tom," I said, "this is an important time in your relationship with your daughter. I suggest that you ask her if she is upset about something. When she responds, listen to her carefully. It is likely that she is feeling a past hurt related to her relationship with you.

"Be very careful not to take what she says personally. You must remember that you are now dealing with the wounded little girl inside your adult daughter. Whether you wanted to or not, you disappointed that little girl many times in the past. Like every other little girl, she tried to capture your attention many times, but she eventually gave up. The emotional bridge between you and your daughter has been down for a long time. She isn't sure she can trust you. She doesn't have a history of experience to convince her that you are really going to be there for her now. She doesn't yet know that you really have changed. So it is a big risk for her to trust you now."

Tom talked to his daughter, and sure enough, she was upset with him. She told him that because he worked two jobs while she was growing up, she didn't feel as if she had a father at all. Irate, she asked him who he thought he was to come back into her life at this late date.

You can imagine how difficult it was for Tom to hear those words, but he knew they reflected the woundedness of his daughter's heart. He offered a simple reply: "I'm sorry I wasn't there for you when you were younger. I want you to know that I am here for you now. If you really don't want me to call you, I will respect that. You let me know what you want me to do."

For several seconds, Tom's daughter said nothing. Then she said, "It's okay for you to call me. Let's go out for lunch soon."

As in Tom's case, the father's consistency in seeking a relationship with his adult daughter is a major factor in her acceptance of the relationship. When a woman realizes that her father is real—that he isn't just playing a hide-and-seek game—the relationship changes dramatically. When the father simply says, "I'm sorry," he has said something his daughter needs to hear. Of course this doesn't mean that everything about the relationship is suddenly better. It just means there is sufficient emotional closeness to talk safely about issues and feelings. Father and daughter then have a foundation on which to build a relationship.

Reconnecting Following Abuse

It can be especially difficult for a father in recovery to reconnect with an adult daughter if he has ever abused her physically, sexually, or emotionally. In practical terms, a father who has abused his daughter has lost the "right" to have a relationship with her. If he is serious about establishing an emotional and spiritual bond with her, he must learn to respect her boundaries and conditions for the relationship.

Abuse creates intense feelings of terror, so if there is to be any hope of restoration, the daughter must perceive the relationship to be safe. In a safe relationship, the father will respect his daughter's fears and will take her feelings seriously. A father who is safe will make amends to his daughter. This may include asking for forgiveness as well as paying for counseling for her. A father who is safe will recognize that healing and forgiveness are on the daughter's timetable, not his own. He will recognize that she may need to define when, where, and how their relationship will be conducted. These emotional, spiritual, and physical boundaries allow a measure of safety that enables the daughter to heal so that forgiveness and restoration can take place.

There are times, however, when fathers need to set boundaries as well. Sometimes an adult daughter will hold onto her hurt and bring it up over and over again. If this happens, the father doesn't have to be punished repeatedly for past offenses. He can say, "I have said that I'm sorry for what happened. I wish I could make it up to you, but I can't. I can only be the best father I know how to be today. It isn't right for me to be beat up over and over again for something in the past that I am sorry for. Since this particular issue keeps coming up, perhaps we should see a pastor or a therapist together so we can work through it."

No father can maintain this level of safety for his daughter and for himself unless he has a solid commitment to his own recovery. Reconnecting when there is such deep woundedness is no easy thing. The relationship can be volatile, offering great hope one moment and bringing crushing defeat the next. So a father who attempts to build an emotional bond needs to remain sober from all addictions and have adequate support so that he doesn't exit emotionally when the going gets tough. He needs ongoing recovery to remain on track and to keep working toward an improved relationship. Finally, his ongoing recovery shows his daughter that he is genuinely repentant and is serious about being a safe father. Even though the past may have been painful, a father who maintains a feeling connection with what is in his own heart has the potential to at last touch his daughter's heart.

Questions

1. Think about your growing up years and the factors that limited the building of a strong emotional bond between you and your father. In what ways are those factors different today? In what ways is your relationship with your father different today?

2. Describe what you, as an adult daughter, would like your relationship with your father to be like. How realistic are your expectations?

3. If geographic distance or infrequent contact are a part of your situation, what might you and your father do to make the most of your relationship?

4. How can you and your father establish realistic expectations for your healing process?

5. Take a few moments to try to identify times your father may have been reaching out to you, but failed. Thank God that He never fails and that He can help you receive your father's offer of restoration.

CHAPTER 11

Hope for a
Healing Community

*How the community of
Christian women can
promote healing and
nurture the development of
biblical womanhood.*

. . . *I was suddenly reminded of a scene from
childhood: we three stair-step sisters, two years apart in
age, legs dangling in a pew, our shoulders hunched over in
fear, as if awaiting a blow. The preacher shouts: "It was
Eve who ate that apple from the Tree of the Knowledge of
Good and Evil. And in going against God's will, in eating
the fruit poisoned with mortality, that woman condemned
us all to exile from God's Garden. She listened to the snake
and her own sinful self, instead of her sweet Lord!" We
shuddered, we three terrified sisters, little descendants of
Eve.*

*It was 1958, and we three little sinners were living in
Montana. . . . At Sunday School, our teacher, as if sens-*

ing the unbroken, fine horse flesh of such high-strung fillies, would glare at us girls as if her lectures were lassos. "Little women have to work especially hard for our Lord's redemption. We were the first in all creation to go against His divine will."

Sometimes it seemed hopeless to a nine-year-old. As the eldest sister, I was often utterly bewildered when the younger ones asked me to explain these sermonettes, as our teacher modestly called them.

"Do you think God will ever forgive us for eating that stupid apple?" my middle sister once asked me as we loped along the open range.

"Nope," I said, and suddenly felt a strange happiness within. At that moment I knew that, no matter what I did, as long as I was female I would always be Eve's daughter. I somehow intuited that being forgiven by this angry Father God might be the same as being broken—the sharp bit of blame always turning me this way and that. Better to be a wild filly with no righteous rider.

That day, when I felt the happy hopelessness of an unforgiven female, I wondered if this feeling was an echo of the still, small voice the preacher was always talking about. But when I asked my Sunday School teacher whether my still, small voice belonged to me or to God, she corrected me soundly. "Nothing about you belongs to you," she pronounced. "Except for your sin."

After that I kept my voice quiet . . . .

. . . I wondered what might have happened if my sisters and I had been blessed with a Sunday School teacher who rocked us in her strong arms, mothering our minds and our souls, telling us stories of women in the Bible who were not harlots or temptresses or slaves. . . .[1]

This excerpt from a tragic, true-life story brings great sadness to my heart. It is a story about wounded sisters—women who have been wounded by their relationship with their earthly father, by life in a not-so-perfect family, by their experience of a shame-filled Christianity, and by the abortion debate. These wounds have led each woman to make painful choices in life, and each still carries the burden of that hurt. Their story touches the wounds of all women.

The author begins by relating a conversation she had with her mother, who at age forty-one had thought she was pregnant and asked her college-student daughter where she might get an abortion. During their talk, the daughter learned that early in her marriage her mother had aborted a baby boy, but that his twin sister had survived. Until that day, the author did not know that she was an abortion survivor. The author goes on to reveal that both she and her younger sister experienced unwanted pregnancies. The author miscarried; her sister had an abortion. Interestingly, she is a pro-choice advocate and her sister, who has never forgiven herself for having an abortion, actively lobbies for the pro-life cause. Through the article, the author shares about their opposing positions and their search for healing. She looks to the feminine spirituality of ancient pagan religions and Native American ritual to "heal the wounds of my fundamentalist childhood," while her sister strives to work out her redemption and healing through anti-abortion activism and strict adherence to Christian fundamentalism. Both women still live in pain.

A Need for Healing

The heartbreaking tragedy of this story is that many women, like the author and her sisters, have suffered deep wounds from a Christian culture that has shamed women. Rather than nurturing women like Esther who can take a powerful stand in a dangerous world, much teaching within the Christian culture has produced women who are mired in shame, poor self-esteem, damaged boundaries, and a lack of personal identity and worth. These wounds have set up women for abusive relationships and addictions that ultimately lead to death. In addition, these wounds have unintentionally contributed to the tragedy of abortion. This is a far cry from a biblical view of feminine.

Imagine for a moment how life might have been different if these two sisters had had "a Sunday school teacher who rocked us in her strong arms, mothering our minds and our souls." What if they had been mothered by a whole community of women who listened to their fears, hurts, and shame, and nurtured their wounded hearts? What if those little girls had a pastor who communicated the worth of women and revealed to them an unwavering identity in Christ? What if these sisters each saw herself as a precious child of God? A sinner, yes, but one who has been made a saint because the Savior sacrificed Himself for her sin so that no more sacrifice would be required.

Jesus was very protective of the souls of children. I do not think He tolerates well the spiritual, emotional, physical, or sexual abuse of children that has taken place within the Christian culture. If He were physically walking on the earth today, I have a hunch He would go into our churches and say, "Why are you wounding My children with shame? My Church is to be a safe place for all of My children to heal and grow." If we are to truly be Christ's community on earth, one of the things we must ask ourselves is whether ours is a theology of shame or a theology of God's overflowing grace that brings healing and is capable of nurturing all of God's children to full maturity.

What's a Father to Do?

We began this book with the story of a father and his daughter who lived in a dangerous culture. It was a society that did not value life, particularly the life of Jews. Life in our world today isn't terribly different. Earlier in this century we witnessed Hitler's attempt to annihilate Jews because he viewed them as less than human. More recently we have witnessed attempts to wipe out the unwanted in the former Soviet Union, Afghanistan, Iraq, Iran, Bosnia-Herzegovina, Croatia, Serbia, South Africa, and a number of other countries and communities. In our own nation, we find it acceptable to end the life of the unborn simply because they are inconvenient.

What does this have to do with fathers and daughters? Much. We no longer have the luxury of passive Christianity. Christian television, books, radio, and tapes are no substitute for active involvement in the Christian community and the culture at large. We need fathers who are spiritually and emotionally alive and live with an intimate connection with the heart of God. We need fathers who feel the grief of abortion, child abuse, homelessness, divorce, and poverty as deeply as Mordecai felt the grief of King Xerxes' edict. We need fathers who realize that the dangers we face are truly matters of life and death. We need fathers who, from the depths of their hearts, plead with God for mercy and deliverance.

We need fathers like Mordecai who feel what it means for their children to live in a dangerous world. We need fathers who, out of the passion of their hearts, will reach out to touch the hearts of their daughters and sons as well as the hearts of children in the church and surrounding community. We need fathers who will work diligently to build an emotional and spiritual bridge to their children. We need fathers who will be painfully honest and unfailingly supportive of their daughters and sons. We need fathers and mothers who will unite with their daughters and sons as a community of people who can make a difference. We need fathers who are bold and wise warriors and who teach their children not only how to survive but also challenge them to stand and fight when necessary.

Fathers such as this cannot rise up from within the Christian community until we address the woundedness that permeates our families, our churches, and our culture. Although the church is in a stronger position to do this now than it was ten years ago, we have a way to go to enable the Church to truly to be a community of healing. The Christian community must become a safe place for the wounded and abused to rise up from the ashes of their past without the shame of perpetual condemnation. It must be a place where those who have been wounded and those who are immature can be nurtured into strong, dignified warriors for the cause of Christ.

This is why the story of Esther and Mordecai is so exciting to me. It illustrates what can happen in a daughter's life when her father is emotionally and spiritually available to her. It shows the unyielding power and strength of a godly woman. It also shows the power of a spiritual community that will sacrifice to nurture and support those who have been called to take a risky stand. Through their story we see in a practical way how a daughter is nurtured and progresses into a fully mature, adult woman.

As a father, I want my daughters to grow up to be strong and capable women of God. I want them to grow up with a strong sense of their identity in Christ and an intimate knowledge of Him. I want them to be able to identify and express what is on their hearts. I want them to believe that their feelings, opinions, and dreams are important. I want them to have a strong sense of self-esteem—an unshakable confidence in who they are physically, emotionally, and spiritually. I want them to set secure boundaries that protect them from harm. I want them to be able to deal with life as it comes to them, without the temptation to survive through fantasy or addiction. I want them to stand free from the shackles of shame and walk as women who are proud and confident.

What I desire for my daughters is something my wife and I cannot accomplish alone. It is something no parents can do alone. Such a solid foundation and potential for growth requires a strong reliance on God and the involvement of a healing community. This community starts with grandfathers, grandmothers, aunts, and uncles, but even the extended family is not enough. This healing community includes family friends, but friends and family are not enough. The whole church community—mentors, disciplers, pastors, Sunday school teachers—needs to be involved as well. God uses all of these people to nurture the spiritual and emotional development of strong and godly women.

A Community of Lifelong Support

If the evangelical Christian church is going to touch the hearts of women, if it is going to nurture women like Esther who have the potential to change their world, we need to change. God did not create women to carry the burden of Eve's sin; He created women to be daughters of the living Savior. He has given women heads that think, strong bodies that carry them through life, hearts that feel, and unique gifts that enable them to accomplish what God wants them to do. He has created their bodies as a precious temple that is capable of nurturing new life. We would do well to affirm, honor, and nurture these aspects of womanhood within the Christian community.

In order to do this, we need to examine our attitudes and beliefs about women and dispense with the shame-filled, unbiblical teaching that holds so many in bondage. We need to honor and affirm that which God has created as feminine. Those of us who are fathers need to face the wounds of our own hearts and open ourselves to God's healing so that we may touch the hearts of our daughters. Finally, we would do well to envision and develop a women's community within the context of the local church that will nurture the hearts of all little girls as they grow into womanhood. If we encourage the development of a strong, loving, and healing women's community, we will strengthen the whole Christian community.

So if you will, envision with me what it would be like if the Christian community were to be a place where a woman's feminine nature is honored, affirmed, and nurtured throughout her life. Envision the inner strength a woman who is part of this kind of emotionally and spiritually healing community would have as she approached life. Envision the impact she would have on her world.

Imagine the potential for spiritual strength when young girls are brought into a community of women who model integrity and valor. Imagine women who are connected with their feelings who hold them and teach them what it means to be a woman of God. Imagine women teaching young girls about Hannah and her earnest prayer to God, Abigail and her bold confrontation of David, Ruth and her faithful support of Naomi, as well as Delilah and her treachery, and Bathsheba and her adultery with David. Can you feel the tremendous spiritual potential and expression that is possible within the context of a vibrant, alive, and honest women's community?

When a girl reaches puberty, imagine the community of Christian women celebrating with her as she changes from little girl to young woman. Imagine what it would be like if a community of women acknowledged her God-given potential to give birth and impressed upon her the honor and responsibility of her new status. The changes in her body would be affirmed as she steps into womanhood with dignity and honor rather than fear and shame. Women of all ages would stand with her mother and father, helping her approach her future with hope and safety.

The community of women can help her develop appropriate boundaries with men, teaching her how to distinguish between men who are safe and those who are dangerous. They can affirm her worth, helping her listen to and act upon the voice from within her that says "caution." They can strengthen her identity and enable her to face the fears of abandonment and rejection rather than seeking the fragile security of a relationship with a destructive young man. They can teach her the disciplines of prayer and the importance of studying God's Word so that she can be empowered and strengthened by her heavenly Father throughout her life.

When a young woman graduates from high school, imagine her celebrating this milestone within the community of Christian women. With the joy of this celebration, the community of women can bless her next steps in life. They can make a solemn commitment to pray for the young woman, upholding her before her heavenly Father.

Imagine this young woman being buoyed up by the phone calls, visits, and letters she receives from these women as she walks her first lonely, challenging months at college. Imagine the strength in which she can walk knowing that a whole community of women cares about her and will support her. Imagine how it would be for her to feel safe in sharing her challenges and struggles as well as her joys and successes with a community of women who are close to her. Imagine what it would be like for her to have the support of other women when she faces the emptiness and loneliness of relationships that come to an end. Imagine the comfort of having an understanding shoulder to cry on in those times of grief, fear, and confusion.

When a woman (whether she is in her twenties or her fifties) obtains her first job, consider how empowering it would be if she was surrounded by women who delight in her success and support her through the wisdom of their experience. Surrounded by a community of women who know her and love her, she would be encouraged and challenged to do her best and also be cautioned about the dangerous and destructive pitfalls she may face along the way. She could be encouraged to have good boundaries so that she is not treated in a demeaning manner, paid less than she is worth, or overworked by her employer. Women who know her will be able to confront her if she is pursuing a path toward burn out. Women who know her abilities will be able to encourage her if she pursues her own business opportunities. Women who love her and respect her as a child of God would be able to uphold her if she fails along the way.

Imagine if the whole community of women were available to celebrate and nurture a young woman when she announces her engagement. In the months, weeks, and days before her wedding, the women could gather around her and prepare her for what lies ahead. They could set aside time to bless her, share experiences from their marriages, and pray for her. Perhaps they would have a celebration in which she is welcomed into the sisterhood of married women.

This sense of community support opens the door for a woman to share her frustrations in her marriage, her joys, her hopes for the future. She is not alone or abandoned as she enters this new phase of her life because she can feel the committed love and support of other women. She can benefit from the wisdom of a community of women as she discovers that marriage is a lifelong process. They can help her understand the ebb and flow of intimacy and growth in her relationship with her husband.

And if she announces that she is pregnant, she has a whole community of women with whom to celebrate and on whom she can depend. As her body changes, they can help her feel the beauty of what is happening within her body. If her baby does not live because of miscarriage, she has a community of women who affirm the reality of her loss. If her baby dies shortly before or after birth, she is surrounded by caring arms in which she can weep. When her baby is born, the community of women can pray for her, call her, make meals for her family, and support her in whatever way she needs.

During those early months of motherhood, another initiation can take place in which she is blessed with respect and honor. The importance of this step in her life is recognized, and the women of the community renew their commitment to support her. They may step in to care for her baby when she is exhausted and depressed. They may listen as she seeks to understand the changes in her relationship with her husband.

If the woman faces infertility, the community of women can surround her with love and affirmation. They can comfort her in her grief. They can support her as she struggles with questions of her identity. They can listen as she tries to make decisions regarding treatment options and perhaps faces disappointment month after month.

If a woman comes to terms with the horror of an abortion experience, the women of the Christian community can receive her with love and can support her as she goes through the process of forgiveness and healing. This process is so much easier when a woman has the support of others who, without self-righteous judgment, will listen to her story, weep with her, mourn with her, hold her up, and pray with her.

So often women in the Church who have had abortions suffer tremendous shame. Feeling worthless, they feel they will never be accepted if their secret is known. This is a wound not only in the woman's relationship with the Christian community, but in her relationship with God the Father. When a woman receives forgiveness and healing, she is lifted up like a new person. She understands God's grace and love at a depth that most people never understand. Rather than being exiled from God and His people, she has much to give.

When a woman who is part of a vibrant community of godly women grows older and her body and hair color changes, she may grieve the loss of her youth, but she also enters into a very important role. She grows into the role of elder within the women's community. This is not a position to be taken lightly. It is a position of honor, wisdom, and strength. It means that she has been empowered through the experience of life and her walk with God to prepare younger women for what lies ahead. The older she becomes, the more she has to give.

And when her time on earth is over, there will be grieving among her family, friends, and the women she has loved and nurtured. Her loss will, for a time, leave an emptiness within the women's community of her church. Another woman will be called to step into her place. Yet the sadness of her loss leads to celebration because this woman of God has taken her final step of initiation and completed her journey in perfect relationship with her heavenly Father.

I do not see this as a dream, a fantasy that can never happen. I see it as a foundation for ministry that will change the hearts of women and will change the Church. I see a community of women who commit themselves to lifelong spiritual growth, brutal honesty, spiritual and emotional intimacy, and unfailing support of one another as a vehicle of healing. Within the Church community, I see women finding healing for the wounds of their fathers. I see those wounds of the heart filled with a deeper and more vital connection with the heavenly Father.

Questions

1. In what ways has the Christian community (particularly the community of Christian women) affirmed, supported or shamed you? What has been the impact of these experiences on your feminine and spiritual identity?

2. What do you need from your Christian community to help reshape that view and encourage you toward godly womanhood?

3. How can the contemporary Christian community provide the nurture fathers need in order to be the kind of men God desires them to be?

4. Do you have a committed group of Christian women with whom to share your life?

5. Take a few moments to reflect on the lessons you've learned through this book. Ask God to continue to minister understanding of these issues to your heart and thank Him for His perfect fatherhood of you.

NOTES

Chapter 1
1. Adapted from the first chapter of the book of Esther. Quotations are from Esther 1:18-20 (NIV).
2. Esther 2:7 (NIV).
3. Told in Genesis 27.
4. Told in Genesis 43, 44, and 45.
5. Told in Genesis 4.
6. Secunda, Victoria, *Women and Their Fathers* (New York: Delacorte Press, 1992) p. 7.
7. Adapted from Esther 2:1-11, quotations from NIV.
8. Scull, Charles, Ph.D., editor *Fathers & Sons and Daughters: Exploring Fatherhood, Renewing the Bond* (Los Angeles: J.P. Tarcher, 1992) p. 99.
9. Secunda, p. 9.
10. Ibid.

Chapter 2
1. The descriptions of father-daughter relationships I have used are an adaptation of the work of Barbara Goulter and Joan Minninger, Ph.D. Their concept of father-daughter relationships is presented in *The Father-Daughter Dance* (New York: G.P. Putnam's Sons, 1993).

Chapter 4
1. Adapted from Esther 2:8-20, quotations from NIV.
2. Adams, Kenneth M. Ph.D. *Silently Seduced: When Parents Make Their Children Partners* (Deerfield Beach, Florida: Health Communications, Inc., 1991) pp. 9-10.
3. Esther 2:11 (NIV).

Chapter 5

1. Adapted from Esther 2:19-4:3, quotations from NIV.
2. Joel 1:13 (NIV).
3. Adapted from Esther 4:4-8, quotations from vv. 6-8 (NIV).
4. Esther 4:11 (NIV).
5. Esther 4:13-14 (NIV).

Chapter 6

1. Adapted from Judges 4:1-22, quotations from NIV.
2. Adapted from Proverbs 31:10-31.
3. Proverbs 31:10, (NIV).
4. Millet, Craig Ballard, *In God's Image* (San Diego: LuraMedia, Inc., 1991) pp. 25-27.
5. Proverbs 31:11-12 (NIV).
6. Proverbs 31:13-15 (NIV).
7. Proverbs 31:16 (NIV).
8. Proverbs 31:17 (NASV).
9. Proverbs 31:18, 20-23 (NIV).
10. Proverbs 31:25-26 (NIV).

Chapter 7

1. Adapted from Esther 4:1-5:1, quotation from NIV.
2. Esther 4:13-14 (NIV).
3. Esther 4:15-17 (NIV).
4. Adapted from Esther 5:1-3, quotation from v. 2 (NIV).
5. Esther 5:8 (NIV).
6. Esther 7:3-6 (NIV).

Chapter 8

1. Author is known but chooses to remain anonymous. Used by permission.
2. Genesis 2:24.
3. John 5:1-9.
4. For further information on healing from the father-son wound, see Dr. Henslin's book, *Man to Man* (Nashville: Thomas Nelson Publishers, 1993).

Chapter 9

1. From 1 John 1:9.
2. Luke 17:3-4 (NIV).

3. Matthew 18:22.
4. "Forgiving the Unforgivable" by Jean Callahan, *New Age Journal*, September/October 1993, p. 78, which refers to *Getting Well Again*, by Carl O. Simonton, M.D., Stephanie Matthews-Simonton, and James Creighton.
5. Robin Casarjian is the author of *Forgiveness: A Bold Choice for a Peaceful Heart.* Quotation is taken from "Forgiving the Unforgivable" by Jean Callahan, *New Age Journal*, September/October 1993, pp. 78-79.

Chapter 10
1. Luke 23-24 (NIV).

Chapter 11
1. Brenda Peterson, "Sister Against Sister," *New Age Journal*, September/October 1993, pp. 68, 144.

About the Author

Earl R. Henslin is a licensed marriage, family, and child therapist. His Brea, California practice through Henslin and Associates focuses on marriage, family, and child counseling, and he conducts training sessions and seminars for professionals such as pastors, physicians, and therapists who work in these areas. He holds the doctor of clinical psychology degree from Rosemead Graduate School of Biola University, where he is a part-time instructor. He is a member of the California Association of Marriage and Family Therapists and the Christian Association of Psychological Studies. Dr. Henslin is also Chairman of the Board of Overcomers Outreach, a nonprofit ministry that assists local churches in establishing twelve-step support groups.

Henslin and Associates provides outpatient treatment and networks with different inpatient treatment facilities for the treatment of adults concerned with codependency, incest, alcoholism, drug addiction, eating disorders, sexual addiction, men's issues, and other issues of dysfunctional families. A nationally acclaimed speaker, Dr. Henslin conducts seminars on these issues for churches, Christian Organizations, counseling centers, and businesses. For information concerning treatment programs or seminars, please contact:

Earl R. Henslin, Psy.D., M.F.C.C.
745 S. Brea Blvd., Ste. 23
Brea, California 92621

Overcomers Outreach, Inc.

Overcomers Outreach, Inc., is a nonprofit, Christ-centered ministry dedicated to helping anyone who would benefit from a twelve-step program. The organization also helps churches establish Christ-centered twelve-step support groups. As of this writing, there are 1,000 Overcomers Outreach groups in 47 states and 10 countries. Internationally, Overcomers Outreach is supported by the tax-deductible contributions of individuals who believe in its goals or have benefited from the program.

Overcomers Outreach is not intended to replace such twelve-step groups as A.A., Al-Anon, A.C.A., and so on. Rather, the organization seeks to supplement those programs and assist Christians who are in recovery. Overcomers Outreach views itself as a bridge between the twelve-step community and churches of all denominations. Its founders are Bob and Pauline Bartosch, who based the ministry on their own recovery experience.

If you are interested in starting a Christian twelve-step support group in your church, contact:

Overcomers Outreach, Inc.
2290 W. Whittier Blvd., Ste. A/D
La Habra, CA 90631(310)
697-3994